Wobbly Legs *on a* Firm Foundation

FINDING STABILITY THROUGH LIFE'S CIRCUMSTANCES

Nia Stivers

WESTBOW
PRESS
A DIVISION OF THOMAS NELSON

WestBow Press books may be ordered through booksellers or by contacting:

WestBow Press
A Division of Thomas Nelson
1663 Liberty Drive
Bloomington, IN 47403
www.westbowpress.com
1-(866) 928-1240

Because of the dynamic nature of the Internet, any web addresses or links contained in this book may have changed since publication and may no longer be valid. The views expressed in this work are solely those of the author and do not necessarily reflect the views of the publisher, and the publisher hereby disclaims any responsibility for them.

Any people depicted in stock imagery provided by Thinkstock are models, and such images are being used for illustrative purposes only.

Certain stock imagery © Thinkstock.

ISBN: 978-1-4497-1557-1 (sc)
ISBN: 978-1-4497-1559-5 (hbk)
ISBN: 978-1-4497-1558-8 (e)

Library of Congress Control Number: 2011926678

Printed in the United States of America

WestBow Press rev. date: 04/14/2011

To my mother, my biggest fan

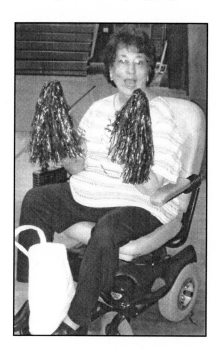

Acknowledgements

Writing this book has been an adventure, and several people have willingly jumped on the "adventure train" with me. I would like to thank them, although it seems I cannot find the words to suffice.

To my husband, who allowed me to take root on the couch during this entire writing process, I love you, I love you, I love you. You inspire me to be a better person. When I look at you and what we have, my eyes are turned toward heaven in thanksgiving for this love He has given us. I believe He truly created you just for me. Love always.

To my mother, you have always been fanatical about everything I have done, whether that was writing my ABC's or writing this book. Your steadfast confidence in me has allowed me to believe in myself. So many times as I wrote, I realized how blessed the life that you and Daddy gave Valerie and me was. Thank you for giving us a happy childhood. I would not be who I am today without that upbringing.

To my sister Valerie, you are the selfless one. I guess it started with you pushing me to walk when I was a baby, but my whole life you have seemed to propel me forward, reminding me of God's promises along the way. You have given me encouragement, a shoulder to snot on, and side-splitting laughter. I always know I will have a good time as long as you are with me. Thanks for sucking all the good genes out of Mama; at least I got a book and good handicap parking out of the deal!

To those who spent countless hours helping me correct grammar mistakes and content errors, which I was ashamed of...being an English teacher and all, I appreciate you: Betty McCraw, Greg Whitcher, sister Val, and dearest friend and my godly role model Julie Foster. Thank you for your wisdom. Thank you for your encouragement. Thank you for helping me reach others for His kingdom purposes.

Brooke Bell, thank you for screaming in my face that weekend at Women of Faith. You have believed in my story (and remembered every detail) for a lot longer than I have. I love my Phi Mu Little Sister!

To my church family and my pastor, Brother Jim Bernard, at First Baptist Church of Bridgeport, you have believed in me and been my pep squad all along the way. You have picked me up and carried me in your arms when I was broken, and you've thrown me up on your shoulders in triumph when God has showered me with His confirmation. I especially want to thank my immediate church family, my choir buddies, who have ridden beside me on my faith rollercoaster all along the way. John and Dana Young, you are a gift to our church and have been a gift to me; thank you for believing in me.

To Carlie and Greg Stephens, thanks for being so excited for me and believing "your girl" could do anything. I cannot begin to tell you how your family has changed me through your love. Thank you for pointing me to Jesus with your lives!

To Gale and Willie Stivers, our long-distance family, although we always wish for more time with you, we are thankful for your continued support and prayers in our lives.

To my dear, sweet friend Alicia Whitcher-Warren, through many a phone call you have listened, and through many a prayer, you have offered me up. Thank you.

To my "Uncle Buster" and "Aunt Susie" Appleton, thank you for believing that there was still something greater to come with the book. Aunt Susie, thank you for helping me work through the shoulder-shaking sobs at the altar and for rubbing my hair.

To Bubba, BJ, and Vayda, thank you for giving me your love and support. You three have blessed our lives...and changed my testimony! We will never be the same because of you...our gifts from God, our "chosen" ones.

To my "babies" at North Sand Mountain School, I believe if I would have told you I was going to run a five-mile race, you would have believed in me. All of you teach *me* so much every day. You love me unconditionally and make me feel "normal." You have celebrated this book with me and begged for more (which I hope was just not sympathy!) My hope for each of you is that you will not waste another day searching for God in your own lives. He's right there waiting with His arms open wide.

To my Lord, my Creator, and my Savior, thank you for writing this book. Thank You for loving me before I loved You back. I love You with all of this wobbly being You created, and I cannot wait to run around in circles when I see Your face in heaven!

Contents

Chapter 1

There is a fuzz bunny at the end of my hallway the size of my weenie dog. Eighty percent of the cooking that is done in my house is completed by my husband. My toenail polish BADLY needs to be redone, and my laundry is beginning to pile up.

At church I sing in the choir but can't figure out where I actually belong. (I sing like a man but can only sing melody, so I sit with the sopranos.) I procrastinate about studying my Sunday School lesson each week, and then the devil runs around in my mind as I try to teach the College and Career Class, making me doubt my knowledge of the Bible, since I wasn't brought up in church. I often do not know basic Bible stories that people allude to when they preach. I cry too much and too often, some would say.

As a family member, I do not give enough. I don't visit enough with my mama or my grandfather. Calling and checking in with people is hard for me as I am on the go all the time. I do not want to be too busy, yet I cannot stop volunteering or saying "yes" to jobs that need to be done. Then, I get so stressed out that I end up crying and being mad at the world for not being able to do the jobs to my specifications; therefore, I have to do it all! I am a registered "Control Freak," I'm sure.

When people ask me for advice I want to solve their problems along with the world's. I feel fairly certain that God needs me to play Jr. Holy Spirit, right? When I or others can't seem to find a reason for what is happening in their lives, I just *have* to find out what God may or may not be thinking. 1 Corinthians 2:9 does not apply to my mind because my mind seems to be able to THINK it IS imagining what God has in store even though the scripture clearly states, "…No eye has seen, no ear has heard, no mind has conceived what God has prepared for those who love Him" (New International Version).

I say all of this to show you that I am so flawed. I am jealous, prideful, slothful, selfish, and I eat way too much, which I think is called gluttony. (I mean, who doesn't wake up thinking about what we will have today for food?) There is absolutely nothing about me that is good or noteworthy. I am filled up with me. Yet somehow, someway, God designed my life, however flawed it may be, to glorify Him. I am amazed that He purposely chose me to go through some of these trials just so I would be different.

As He knit me together in my mother's womb, His mighty fingers pushed down on my shoulders, popped out my shoulder blades, and weakened my legs for the purpose of limping around on this earth and loving Him through it all. He wanted me to laugh at myself and smile at my circumstances, knowing that He has the whole thing we call "life" under His command and His control.

This is my story of how He has and continues to make me whole…

Chapter 2

I am eleven years old. I'm mad because I missed a day of sixth grade for this silly doctor's appointment that started with my dad asking me to "Sit up straight, baby." I was sitting up straight. I was holding my shoulders back; yet to them, something was off. Deep down inside, they already knew what it was.

After a series of tests including muscle biopsies, my mother was diagnosed with Fascioscapulahumeral Muscular Dystrophy when she was in her thirties. By this time, she had already given birth to my ten-year older sister Valerie and me. Now, here in the office for my appointment in Chattanooga, Tennessee, the doctor had given his verdict that there was no need to do further testing and submit me to all that pain. Fascioscapulahumeral Muscular Dystrophy, or FSHD for short, is passed down genetically. What my mother had was also manifesting its symptoms in me, though I was cheerleading and playing softball at the time.

The weakness and drooping in my shoulders and the winged scapula were what my dad had noticed in me when he had encouraged good posture. In that room, sitting on that table blanketed in too-thin paper, I looked to my right and saw my father let his chin drop to his chest. Shoulders began to heave back and forth and choked-back sobs seeped from his throat. My daddy, my six-foot-six, 300-pound superhero had been defeated by a kryptonite that lived inside of me.

My mother did not meet my gaze. She was staring out the window. If she stared long and hard enough, she believed, she could keep her back turned toward the monster in that room. A battle raged inside her own disease-racked body: the enemy of fear forced boulders of sobs to rise in her throat and caused her bottom lip to quiver versus the contender of motherly protection, which gave her a strong desire to take this burden away from my future. "What have I done? This disease is hereditary, starting with me. I've given this to her. I can bear this. It's mine to bear, but her? Oh God, PLEASE take it away from her body. I will take it all." The words that ran through her head were not, however, what came out of her mouth: "We'll fix it, baby. It is gonna be ok." She was trying to convince herself as she reassured me.

Sitting there, I never could begin to understand the sentence that was given to my parents that day. Letters in a too-long word that most people couldn't pronounce would begin to take hold of my life and force me to hobble along, carrying this 100-pound rucksack of feeling "not normal" for the rest of my days. One moment, a few words, a broken daddy, a fighting mad mama, and a ripped apart eleven-year-old girl.

That day the phone rang too much. Family members who were anxious for news never knew that they really didn't want to hear the truth. Mama went to bed, curled in the fetal position, and became angry at God. I have never known why my parents quit going to church after about the time I was five or six years old. Now that I was eleven and we still were not in church, God sure didn't convince my mother on this day that He was what we needed. In other words,

He did not win one for the "God team" that day. Mom avoided answering the phone like she avoided this agonizing truth. Daddy immersed himself in Westerns in the living room to escape reality. Two hours away, Valerie, my twenty-one year old sister, my hero, was being held in her dorm room by her roommates in an attempt to control her racking sobs amongst the objects that were being thrown. I, however, was oblivious to my life-sentence. Sometimes, youthful ignorance is bliss.

The next few months were spent trying to fight off this monster. I would be checked out of school to go back to Chattanooga, a forty-minute drive, for occupational therapy. There, in the floor of TC Thompson's Children's Hospital, I lay on my belly on a blue mat, trying to pick my arms up off the floor and hold them, suspended in mid-air until the therapist allowed me to collapse them. I crawled the wall with my fingers, inching up, up, up until I could no more. The therapists drew out pictures of various exercises for me to take home, and I would diligently give this Muscular Dystrophy monster the ol' one-two with my squats and arm lifts.

At school, there were no noticeable differences on the outside, at least not in my mind. I believed I was doing a great job hiding my flaws because when you're in middle school, being like everyone else is to be "normal." I cried alone at night in my *My Little Ponies* bed covering, with my face muffled in my Disney character pillow. I asked a God, whom I did not know, yet invariably blamed, "Why me?" My doctor's appointments were secret and there was no mention of my awkward walking among my classmates whom I had known since kindergarten. I did not know that I was just truly in a safe haven of friends and teachers, who knew me so well that they did not pay attention to any differences, and the whole time, I thought I had *them* fooled that there was nothing wrong with me. It wasn't until high school that I knew the secret was out…

Chapter 3

efore band practice one day in the ninth grade, a friend of mine told me that a boy and girl in her class had gotten up in front of the class and mimicked the way I walked for everyone to laugh with in agreement. I was devastated by this because no longer could I blend in with the crowd and just remain unnoticed. Despite my fiery mouth and my love of being the center of attention, I didn't want to lay my weaknesses out on display.

I have to say that I was pretty dog-gone good at making others believe there was nothing different about me. I made myself believe myself! I made all the typical teenage mistakes. I dated a guy that my parents forbid, just to defy them because I thought it was "real love." I didn't pick up the phone (the ones with a cord) to tell my parents where I was or why I was running late. I was dumb, now that I think about it, and the bad part was that I thought I was the smartest thing that ever walked God's green earth. Let me just sidetrack to give you an example of teenage stupidity at its finest…

My best friend in high school was a boy who was a year older than I was. He was a guy whom my mom deemed as no risk to me, and she seemed to realize our friendship. He could drive, so occasionally Mama would let me go somewhere with him. One night, he and I were at his house watching a movie. I looked up to his digital clock, which said it was ten minutes after ten o'clock. Now this makes no difference to you, but to my mom, who had laid down the law of a "ten o'clock curfew" to her now fifteen-year-old daughter, being ten minutes late was equivalent to dead in a ditch. I knew, as my mouth gaped in horror while I stared at that clock, that by now, she was pacing the floors, fingers poised on the phone, talking herself out of calling the police.

We raced out the door, to his car (a Mercury Cougar, which we affectionately named "the Pimp-Mobile"), and down Highway 72, making the ten-minute drive from Stevenson to Bridgeport. As we neared my road in Bridgeport, we were now twenty minutes late. Death was certain for me. Because fifteen-year-old girls are brilliant and conniving, I told my friend to pass the road to my house and go up to the gas station. (Yes, I said "THE" gas station. There's only one, which sits next to the one red light we have in our town.) Once at THE gas station, I proceeded to get out of the car and approach the pay phone with a master plan.

Frantic mother: "Hello?"

Idiot Daughter: "Hey Mama. Ummm, I just wanted to let you know, because I knew you'd be worried, that we stopped in Stevenson at the gas station, and when we came out, you know how his old car is, it just wouldn't start. Never you worry now though. We have it started, that's what took so long, and I'll be home in ten minutes." (Now notice that I said we were in Stevenson. No, we were in my home town of Bridgeport. The way I figured (because I had two brain cells at that age), in the ten minutes we were driving from "Stevenson to Bridgeport," he and I could just ride around some and spend more time together. Great thinking, right?

Lesson #1: Don't mess with my mother, Bea Cox. She doesn't play when it comes to her daughters. To say she was strict would be like calling Cruella de Ville "Mother Teresa."

Frantic mother: "Oh, you're in Stevenson, huh? No need for him to bring you home. You just keep your butt right there. (Except she didn't say butt because we were not right with the Lord then.) I'll be there to get you in ten minutes."

Words ceased to come to my mouth. I looked at my friend, terror filling my eyes, and yelped while dropping the germ-infested pay phone receiver. As I ran to the car, somehow he knew to run also. I told him that she was coming TO STEVENSON to get me. We weren't there, remember? To add to that, if we headed back to Stevenson, we would risk passing her on the way! The back roads were our only hope, although they typically took longer than the highway, and every second would matter here. My friend roared the Cougar to life, and we zipped down the back roads, dodging whatever 'possums might dare to cross our path. Somehow, (and I cannot say it was by God's grace because I don't think He blesses running to outwit your parents,) we made it to Stevenson with two minutes to spare before my mother pulled into the gas station parking lot, where his car had ostensibly had trouble starting. She beckoned with that one index finger motion that mothers do for me to get into the car lest I never breathe another breath here on earth. On the way home, she lectured me about responsibility, and for punishment, she made me call all of my percussion friends from the band and cancel the get-together I had planned for us at my house that weekend. (She never knew the truth behind this story until I was in college and emailed a story I had written about it to my sister Valerie, who happened to read the story to my mom. Ummm, hmmm. *Sure* she did not realize Mama had no idea.)

Oh well, now you get the stupidity that oozed from my ears. I was a typical teenage girl, and I worked hard to emphasize "typical."

In tenth grade, I dated a guy who had a four-wheeler. I loved to ride it, as I never had a four-wheeler growing up. One day, however, I jumped on the four-wheeler and couldn't get my left foot to pop up the gear shift. It seemed that the top of my foot was too weak to apply the upward pressure needed to shift gears. I did not know then, that what had happened overnight, it seemed, was called "foot drop." It was the beginning of walking and slinging my foot out in front of me to keep my toes from dragging the ground. It was the beginning of tripping and falling. It was the beginning of more stares and more jeers. It was the end of the denial, and the beginning of my anger towards the disease.

Chapter 4

I learned in a Bible study once that anger often happens because we feel threatened. Yeah, I guess I was threatened alright. Threatened to be labeled as "weird" or "different" in school. Threatened that I would never play softball, run again, or choose a marching instrument in the band. Those were the biggies then.

As life went on, my anger was directed at much larger issues. I was robbed of ever feeling a child move inside of me. Anger built up because I couldn't just go on any excursion a cruise has to offer. When looking at the cruise brochure and reading the descriptions of the island excursions, I not only had to look at the dollar sign icons but also had to look for only one of the little physical activity man icons. (Three icon men usually meant you were going to climb a waterfall or something adventurous like that.) Not me. I had to stick to the ground, and that ground better have been level.

Simple things that people take for granted, such as choosing cruise excursions, can prove difficult for me. Here, Jason and I snorkel in Mexico.

I'm angry that people stare at my legs when I walk through the mall. It makes me feel like I'm just a pair of wobbling, foot slingin' legs (which are, by the way, built a lot like upside-down tapered candles with several wax dents at the top). I have no head or torso to those on-lookers. I'm just the legs. I want to scream, "I am a person! I am not just this disease! There is more to me if you'd just look up!"

In high school, I used to walk around with a smart-mouthed response ready for anyone who dared make fun of me. I became proficient in sarcasm, which I believe is one of my greater talents, and unfortunately, began to look for others' weaknesses, so as to be ready to counterattack their own personal deficiencies.

One time, my mother and I were in a restaurant. As I got up to take our tray, I walked by a man and his family. As I wobbled on by, I saw the man nudge his wife and say, "Y'all watch this. Watch the way this girl walks." I swear that I felt my blood pressure start in my toenails and shoot out the pores of my scalp.

12

"*What did you say?*" I demanded through my gritted teeth as I limped up to the edge of his table.

He sat with his head down, no eye contact at all. (It was probably a good thing because I probably would have punched him in the eyeballs had they laid their gaze on me. I'm telling you, I was feisty back then.)

Mama wheeled up about this time, "Nia! What are you doing?"

"Hold on a second, Mama. This man has something he needs to say to me."

Nothing but crickets could be heard there in the ol' corner booth. No wise cracks from Mr. Man. No stares. I felt triumphant; but the emotion was fleeting once I went to any other public establishment.

Another time I was in a department store. Every time I went down an aisle, there was this man. I began to feel that we weren't just shopping for the same items, so I purposely went across the store in some random aisle of cleaning products. Guess who? There he was. My assistant shopper/starer.

As luck would have it while I was shopping and needed to stand there awhile, I had to go to the bathroom. Wouldn't you know that it was one of those really scary ones in the back of the warehouse? As I eased my way around boxes and inventory and went into the restroom, I began to wonder. "What if I come out of this stall, and he's just standing there in front of the sinks? What is a handicapped girl's game plan going to be? I could scream like a banshee while stabbing him in the eyes with my car keys." Ok, I'm prepared. Click. I opened the door and stepped to the sink to wash my hands. No man. Whew, I'm good.

Feeling safe, I opened the door of the restroom to walk back out into the warehouse. When I opened the restroom door, TADA, there he was!

"What's wrong with your leg, girl?" he slurred.

Really? Really? Are you serious? This is what he's been following me around for? I was more than a little insulted. I was furious at his *stupidity and his gall. I actually thought of telling him that I had a horrible car accident and my leg was maimed. No, maybe I was a sports star and had injured it in the big game. Oh, oh, or maybe, I had a wooden leg, like a pirate, and the termites had been chewing on it.*

Instead I said, "Well, if you MUST know, I have Muscular Dystrophy."

"Oh," he said. "I'm sorry. I was just wondering."

Now there have been a lot of things in my life that I have wondered about when I have seen people out in the world. Is she dating that much older man? Why do all the druggies have a litter of babies that they cannot take care of? Is she anorexic? How can he stand that nagging wife in the grocery store? BUT I DO NOT GO UP TO THEM AND ASK! Socially disabled. That is what those people are. I'm convinced.

No one wants to be stared at, no one wants to be treated differently or questioned, and no one wants to put up with, "Oh, bless your heart, hon. You're crippled." Well, thank you very much for blessing my heart, but no, I do not consider myself crippled. I can't speak for everyone who may be "different" or "handi-*capable*," but I know my own limitations and setbacks. I don't need anyone to point them out and make them more obvious than they are. So when you're walking into your local grocery store, and you see someone with Cerebral Palsy or someone who is blind, look the other way. Not in shame or disgust, but just to simply make them feel like anyone else who is coming out of the store. Be the ONE person in their day who did not treat them like a leper. It threatens our dignity and our pride, and that leads to anger.

ife changed my tenth grade year when I was fifteen years old. It was the year the Lord placed me in His hand, and the beginning of many future years of my dancing along the edges of His fingers, dangerously close to falling.

Valerie and I had the most supportive and nurturing parents while growing up.

I had the greatest family I could ever ask for growing up. My mom and dad's salary together was what I make now as a teacher, which everyone knows is not that significant. (Example: An assistant manager at a fast food restaurant made more than I did when I graduated from college with my Bachelor's degree.) Although my parents were careful with our money, whenever an opportunity presented itself at school, such as a field trip or class project, they made sure I was involved. They came to all the football games to watch as I played the bells and the xylophone on the sidelines while the marching band exercised their strong legs behind me. They made me do my homework as soon as I came home from school. My family encouraged me to work a part-time job after school to begin paying for any brand name clothes I wanted, so that I would learn to appreciate what I had and the value of hard work. They pushed my sister and me to become strong, independent women, who could take care of ourselves. In the midst of a million and one moral qualities that my parents instilled in us, one major aspect was absent: God.

My parents had gone to church when I was little. I was in children's plays and remember snatching candy off the walls that had been taped up in the fellowship hall during our Halloween party. Something happened, however, that made my parents quit attending church while I was in elementary school. I think there was a rift in the church or my parents got their feelings hurt or whatever, but my mother doesn't even remember. With all due respect to my sweet parents, that pride and "self" that they wore then kept my sister and me from knowing the true lessons we needed to learn. I needed to know that God thought I was beautiful and that He doesn't make mistakes. It would've been important that I knew that He "knit me together in my mother's womb" because that might have kept me from being angry with Him, the disease, my mother for passing it on to me genetically, and others for staring. I would have known that His love was unconditional and that it was really all I ever needed.

I have never been angry or upset with my parents about our absence from church. We all walk in the dark from time to time, and we all fall for the devil's lies. I'm sure my parents thought they were raising intelligent, proactive women just fine on their own. But as God would have it, He began to woo me to Himself. The concept of that is just amazing to me. He loved me so much, back when I was saying "Why God?" to Him, back when I didn't know about His birth, what resurrection was, or that He had a purpose and a plan for this disease, He still wanted me to love Him. He'd already chosen to love me thousands of years ago when He allowed His son to die in my place. I never knew God's love was behind that invitation to Vacation Bible School...

I had a friend who was struggling in her young faith. She, at least, was going to church and trying to do better. I didn't know I was doing wrong. I guess that's why I didn't feel uneasy about going to a high school version of Vacation Bible School with her one night during the summer. We were also having band camp for two weeks, so having the energy to go to VBS that night was a miracle in itself.

I don't remember what the VBS lesson was about that night. I do, however, remember how I felt after we'd left the fellowship hall where our study had been to go back into the church where the preacher could talk to us. I don't even remember what he said. I just remember standing there during a song, white-knuckling the pew in front of me, and knowing that I had never gone to an altar to pray before. I didn't know Jesus "as my personal Lord and Savior." I didn't really even know what that meant. I felt like there was an empty spot inside of me that maybe walking to the front of that church would fill, but I was too scared. Walk up in front of all those other kids? I think not. I would just keep feeling what I was feeling and wondering what I was wondering.

At home one night the next week, I asked my mother about the feeling I had gotten when the preacher invited us to come and pray.

"How would I know? What does it mean to be saved?" I asked.

For the first time in my life that I remember, my mother talked to me about God. She said that she, my dad, and my sister had all "accepted" Jesus as their Savior and that when the time came, I would just know. She said, "It feels like a strong feeling that you just need to go and pray. At the same time, you may feel like you're scared and want to run away. Nia, you will just know when you know."

Sometimes it amazes me to think of conversations and points in my life that I remember. Why do some memories stay and some leave our brains? For as many good conversations as I'd had with my mother, this one was divine. It was a pre-op appointment before my heart transplant.

There was no coincidence in the fact that a night or so later the preacher from the church where I had gone to VBS just happened to show up at my house. He said I had filled out a card with my address on it while I was there, and I had checked that I would like to know more about getting saved. Wow! Did I even remember doing that?

As the preacher walked into the living room of our house and my father muted the Western that was on the TV, my mother came in from the den to hear what was being said. I remember him sitting knee to knee with me in the juxtaposed chairs. He held his Bible in his hands and read highlighted scripture to me.

"Do you know what that means?" he asked after reading Romans 10:9-10--"That if you confess with your mouth Jesus as Lord, and believe in your heart that God raised Him from the dead, you will be saved; for with the heart a person believes, resulting in righteousness, and with the mouth he confesses, resulting in salvation."

"Uh huh," I agreed. "It means that I just need to believe Jesus is God's son and that He died for me." (I had no idea about the righteousness part or how that would all work itself out.)

"Nia, do you want to be saved?" he asked.

My heart beat out of my chest. My hands were sweating. Finally, finally, someone had asked me a question that my soul had been trying to break lose inside of me. I knew. There was no doubt. I wanted Jesus in my life. I wanted to go to heaven.

"Yes!" I practically shouted.

We knelt together on our seventies-style olive green carpet that was patterned to look like heads of broccoli. I lay my face in the chair where my mother always sat to open her Christmas presents. There, I received the ultimate gift: salvation. I had done nothing to deserve it. I would later learn that I could do nothing to take it away. I asked the Lord to come into my heart and save me, and as I ended my prayer to the sniffles and snorts of my mama and daddy, I felt like an electric blanket had been placed around my shoulders. I was finally whole and in His hand.

Chapter 6

 he next day during our band camp, I cussed. The drum
major, a friend of mine who was already a Christian, said,
"Nia, congratulations! I heard the good news about your
getting saved last night. Looks like some things have not changed
yet though."

Great. My first of many mess-ups living life on the ol' Christian
witness stand. In that one moment I felt that I had so disappointed
God that I was never going to be able to live this new life. Now, I'm
not holding the drum major at fault. The sad part is, I'm afraid that
in later years, I would also call new Christians out on their obvious
sins, and I am not sure it has always come out as it was explained
in 2 Timothy 3:16 (The Message): "All Scripture is God-breathed
and is useful one way or another—showing us truth, exposing our
rebellion, correcting our mistakes, training us to live God's way."
Instead, I did it from my own self-righteousness, not from scripture
and not always in love. I am better at following the scripture in
Romans 7:15 (The Message) "What I don't understand about myself
is that I decide one way, but then I act another, doing things I
absolutely despise."

My new relationship with God was a seed planted but never watered, shined upon, or cultivated. I never found a church. I did not even look. I continued on my merry way feeling confident of my salvation and my ticket to heaven, but never knowing all the promises that had been made to me. I had accepted Jesus as my Savior but not my Lord. It was going to take a while before I realized I needed both.

Chapter 7

As a tenth grader, I had a crush on a boy named Jason Stivers. He played basketball, had beautiful auburn red hair, and my family knew his family to be a good one. (This was a far cry different than the boys I had previously dated. Wait. That's an understatement. I had dated a boy who had bitten me when he got unnecessarily jealous. Yes, if the previous boy was a pit bull, then Jason was a Labrador.) All the while I had my crush on Jason, the jealous boy I had dated in the ninth grade was scaring off any new prospects. I did, finally, start to date a very nice boy, a football player, who happened to be mutual friends with Jason. I tried to keep my eyes turned toward my new boyfriend and not my old crush, Jason, who was oblivious to me. As life would happen, one night after a football game, my football player boyfriend I had then said there was no room in his family's car for me to ride home with them because another girl was riding home. Well, well, well. Do you think he had just broken up with me? I was shocked, mad, and stranded. Thank God I could ride back on the band bus.

I was heartbroken for the next several days. It was my time to experience that snot-slingin', "I'll-never-love-again" rite of passage for teenagers. During my time of grief, I received a phone call one night. I remember my sister bringing the phone into the room while I mouthed "Who is it?" My heart skipped a beat because I thought it was my ex boyfriend, calling to tell me what a horrible mistake he had made. Oh, no, it was even better! It was my crush Jason! He had called to check on me after the breakup; that was all. (Now you may believe he had ulterior motives, but after knowing him like I do, yes, he was just that thoughtful.) What he expected to be a five-minute conversation turned into many nights of one hour and a half conversations. Soon, he asked me to come to his house while he washed his little red Chevrolet S-10. Not that romantic, I know, but I would have watched him scrub a toilet if that meant I could be around him.

Jason was a rule follower, a son infatuated with his mother, and a scaredy cat when it came to being the center of attention or speaking in public. When we would call a local restaurant to place a to-go order, I had to do the calling. He and I got along wonderfully. We were never one of those volatile teenage relationships that broke up every other day.

We were as opposite as could be. I loved being in the spotlight; he took care of things behind the scenes. I was loud and quick to give my opinion; he was quiet, but when he spoke, his opinion was valued. I did not grow up in church; he grew up living in the house with his grandfather, an old-fashioned Baptist preacher, who was one of the finest men I have ever met. I had a sister; he was an only child and the pride of his family. I loved rap and R&B; he taught me to love older rock like Steve Miller Band and Bob Seger and the Silver Bullet Band. Everything about us was opposite, which was great because he was a mystery to me. I was always intrigued.

We "talked" for about two months before we officially started dating. (He had that much respect for his mutual friend and my ex so as not to make him believe we had liked each other while I was still in the relationship with my ex. Jason was better than I was about waiting to date each other...) On November 3, 1996, during our junior year of high school, Jason and I had been on a date and were standing in my garage. He said, "Nia, are you ready to be 'my girl'?" After I picked myself up from the puddle I had oozed into, I said yes, and we kissed.

Jason and I when we were still in high school.
This was before one of our first dates.

It did not take long before I realized that there were some serious differences about this red-headed boy in comparison with any other boy I had dated. *One night we got up to leave our table at a fast food restaurant. He grabbed my plastic tray and took it to the garbage for me. I stood there. I think he thought he'd thrown away something valuable of mine that was on that tray.*

"*What's the matter?*" *he asked.*

Now, what was I supposed to say? "I'm in love with the way you carry my trash?" Yeah, that would have been really cool. So I didn't say a thing. I just grinned, and my heart took notes and gave out bonus points.

One night Jason's family asked him to talk to one of his cousins. She was struggling with drugs at the time, and the two of them had such a connection, that often, Jason was able to calm her down and speak such truth to her that it penetrated the lies she wanted to believe through the drugs. I watched Jason transform that night. I saw him move to protect me from the ugly side of drugs, as I had never experienced being around anyone who was suffering their addictive power. Jason locked me in the truck while he went inside to talk to his cousin, but before leaving me in the safety and warmth of the S-10, I could see that he had morphed into what his cousin would need him to become once he walked through those doors. He was wise, cautious, and overwhelmingly compassionate. He was eaten up with concern for his cousin, and he hoped he would have the right words to jolt her back to reality. I sat in the truck while he was handling matters behind the door of that small apartment. My heart was fearful for him, yet it also was honing in on the characteristics he had just exhibited. Jason was a secure support for his family and would be exactly what a girl with a progressing muscular disease would need.

When we left that night, Jason was worried about his cousin. He couldn't contain his fears and soon his face was wet with those concerns. As he leaned his head over on my shoulder where his arm was already around, he whispered, "I love you. Thank you for being with me tonight. I'm sorry you had to be a part of that."

I did not reply at that moment. I had made up my mind that I would tell him how I felt in my own time. I didn't want it to seem like a "ditto" moment or a "right back at 'cha." So I simply laid my head on top of his and burned that memory into my brain.

That night as he dropped me off, I felt like I could contain it no longer. Yes, I'd had plans of waiting until another time, but as he walked me up the steps in my garage, I turned to face him. "I love you too," I simply said.

Now, although this relationship was blessed because it was different than anything I'd ever experienced, God was not acknowledged as the center of it. We were both saved, but yoking, be that equal or unequal, was not anything we had thought about or understood."Be ye not unequally yoked together with unbelievers: for what fellowship hath righteousness with unrighteousness? And what communion hath light with darkness?" (2 Corinthians 6:14, King James Version). But one of the aspects of this relationship that excited me was the regular church attendance of his family. I thought, "Finally, a good excuse to get to go to church each Sunday!" I knew that something was missing from my life. I was sure of my salvation, yet I still wasn't living my life for Christ because I didn't even know how to begin. Unfortunately, Jason was feeling the opposite about church. He'd been going to church all his life, and he dreaded every Sunday as he was expected to be there. I wasn't brave enough to tell him how I felt because talking about God just wasn't something I'd ever been around or done myself.

I simply began to soak up what I could around Jason's home. Scripture hung on the walls, especially in the kitchen, which was our main meeting ground. "In all your ways acknowledge Him, and He will make your paths straight" (Proverbs 3:6, New International Version) hung over the kitchen table on a tapestry woven to depict a garden path. (Isn't it amazing how we can continue to miss the obvious signs of direction from God?) Jason's grandfather, who was a preacher remember, made me feel like a weenie dog to cheese. Wherever he was, I wanted to be there also. He was funny and had such corny jokes that you could not help but smile. When we would leave to go somewhere, we'd holler, "We're gone!"

His grandfather would reply, "Well turn your hat around backwards so I think you're comin'!"

I loved that man. He studied his Bible at the kitchen table, and often I would sit and ask him questions like "What's a sepulcher?" or "What do you think I should do about this situation, Paw?" I longed to be around him, and he seemed to love me the same, especially when we were having hushpuppy-eating contests. In later years, when his health was failing, I would climb into the hospital bed beside him. He'd say, "There comes 'That girl,'" which was what he had affectionately nicknamed me. He loved me, I loved him, and I loved that Jason had so many of his characteristics.

*Jason's grandfather, Thomas, was my first
model of living life for the Lord.*

Jason was good to his mother, a fiery red-haired petite woman. I've always heard that you can tell how a guy will treat you by the way he treats his mother. I had nothing to fear then. Jason's relationship with his mother taught me to be more patient with my mother. (Because, remember, we had that typical wise mother/idiot teenage daughter thing going on at that time.) I learned from the two of them that having the last word did not really matter. Jason's mother was strong and independent enough to handle work in the business world yet soft and gentle with her son and with me. She would call friends and family while she was shopping to see if they needed any groceries, and even if they didn't place their "order" for their own food, she'd share what she had with them. I noticed that she did not force opinions on us, but instead, led with such an example that we wanted to please her.

Carlie, Jason's mother, is a woman who loves
life and loves taking care of others.

I did not realize then, that even though we weren't in church—well, we were "in church" because they expected us to be in the building—we were learning godly examples from Jason's grandfather, grandmother, stepfather, and mother who were all packed into a little house right across the street from the church where Jason's grandfather preached.

As fairy tale as all this seemed, our relationship was now at a crossroad. We had been together a year and a half, and our senior year was coming to an end. Jason and I had different plans after we left high school. I was going to college, and he would be traveling to work construction as an electrician. My boss at my after-school job said, "Nia, you might as well go ahead and break up with him. What college graduate will want to be with a construction worker? Plus, long distance relationships don't work." Ah, a challenge. This wasn't some high school romance, and we weren't about to let it go. We were going to need each other more than we ever realized, and God had planned how He was going to reveal that to us in the next few years.

Chapter 8

7 ragedy struck our family at the end of my senior year. Our high school band had been invited to play on the White House lawn during the week of spring break. After playing in Washington, D.C., we were then to travel to New York City to tour. My sister went with us as a chaperone. Now, most teenagers would be thinking, "Great, an older sister to go as a tattle tale." It was because my sister and I were ten years apart that we were so close. I looked forward to her going with us on the trip. That meant stolen glances of inside secrets, a reassurance of someone who knew when to tell me to quit pushing myself when I wanted to climb the steps to the crown of the Statue of Liberty with everyone else, and the occasional side-splitting laughter that came after playing our version of "Dueling Banjos" by humming through our noses while strumming the side of our nostrils. (Go ahead. You know you want to try it.) While I looked forward to these events of which I was sure were to come while in Washington and New York, we were unable to foresee the actions that were taking place back in Bridgeport, Alabama. My sister's husband of two years was leaving her. While on the trip, Valerie often expressed to me her worry that something was looming about their relationship.

31

"He's just acting weird," she would say. "He's very short when he talks to me on the phone and is often not home when I call. I just feel like something is wrong."

When we got home from our week-long trip, her husband was gone. He'd left, in return, a note. He wasn't happy. It wasn't her fault. He was sorry. A few lines on a sheet of paper plus a few missing bath towels multiplied by a family that had never experienced divorce equaled devastation and heartbreak; it was an equation that we did not know how to solve.

My sister cried incessantly. My parents were ready to protect her in any way, and I was angered in a way I had not yet experienced. It turns out that he had left her for another woman he had met at the plant where he worked. My sister had formerly been employed there before she got her first teaching position; this was the woman who had taken my sister's job after she left. This was irony at its finest. Guess who else worked at that very place? Me. It was my after school, part-time job. I was a file clerk/office flunky. As I slowly began to realize who the "other woman" was that my former brother-in-law was courting, working there became awful for me. Every deviant thought I had toward my ex brother-in-law or toward the "new woman" had to be suppressed inside of me. I didn't need to lose my job; plus, my mother's wisdom rang true in my ears: "If you mess with crap, you get it on you." In other words, "Don't stoop to their level. Be better than to get down in the muck and wallow with them." (Not the most eloquent words, but it got the point across and has proven true many times in my life.)

I made it through the final months of having to work there before going off to college. Meanwhile, my sister was battling those vultures in our small town who loved the idea of someone else's failed marriage validating their own shortcomings and failures. She was obsessed with wanting her husband back. She had loved being married and had had no intentions of it ending without her consent.

A few times my ex brother-in-law came back home, but it was short lived, and he was usually gone the next day. My mother, father, and I all seemed to be content to stay angry and protective of my sister and her pride. She was in a deep well sitting alone at rock bottom. My family and I guarded the surface by dodging nosey questions, fighting off lies, and pounding in the truth to those who tried to get near her. While we had been looking at each other and at any "enemies" at ground level, she had begun to look up from the well—way up.

My sister started going to church again. Not just any church, but the church my mother and father had originally left. I thought she was crazy, to be honest. The way she talked about God and wrote these scripture down everywhere was foreign to me. I knew that she was saved but was she obsessed? What was wrong with her? My family and I were not very interested in what she had to explain. That's the way it seems to be when others who are close to God remind you how far away you are from Him: conviction. She went on to church without us. Alone she went to discipleship training, conferences, and services. She was finding the Truth of Love after losing what she thought was her true love. "And I pray that you…may have power…to grasp how wide and long and high and deep is the love of Christ, and to know this love that surpasses knowledge—that you may be filled to the measure of all the fullness of God" (Ephesians 3:17-19, New International Version).

One week she asked me to go with her, and the next week she asked again. "Are you crazy?" I asked. "That's the church where all the roo-di-poo (a Southern synonym for "uppity") people go from school. I wouldn't fit in there." I gave in. It was my sister, after all, and she never led me astray. So I went one Sunday morning. I slipped in the door and hoped no one was comparing my Sunday best to theirs because I didn't have many dress clothes. She sat on the front pew. Great, Val. Thanks. Let's just get right here in the front and soak it all up while everyone stares at us. Instead, they hugged us. And you know what? I *believed* their hugs. It felt real. I didn't know the words to the songs, but it was ok because I could bury my face in the hymnal.

Then came the part I dreaded most: the preaching. I had never comprehended a sermon in my life. Yes, I had been convicted enough to be saved when I was fifteen. I'd taken opportunities to go to church with other friends or with Jason, but the "thee's" and "thou's" were still just as confusing as ever. The pastor stood tall, yet he looked the grandfather type. He had a kind smile, and he laughed at his own jokes as he began his sermon. I had an overwhelming desire to hug him the whole time he was behind the pulpit. When he opened his mouth to preach, I leaned in closer on the pew. He spoke softly when he wanted to make a big impact. There was no screaming or yelling, which had always been a little scary to me. He might as well have opened up a children's story book to read while I sat at his feet on a carpet with ABC's on it. I understood every word he said. His real-life examples made perfect sense along with what he explained about the scripture. I could not believe it. This was church, and I had been missing out.

"Brother Jim" Bernard, my pastor, my friend.

I became excited about church like Valerie was. I knew that I never would have darkened the door alone had it not been for her, nor did I ever go alone on a Sunday if she could not. Our excitement wasn't received well by Mama and Daddy when we got home each time. It's not that I believe they weren't happy about our going, I just believe that those ol' hurt feelings that had separated them from that very church were what kept them from wanting to attend with us. Plus, who likes feeling convicted when your daughters are involved in church without you?

My sister's devastation seemed, at the time, to be undeserved. What appeared to be a mistake in her life had caused Valerie to seek help in an untapped resource: the Lord. Now God was taking His mighty hands, and, as one rakes crumbs off a counter, was scooping together the ashes of that broken marriage, which Valerie now believes fell apart because it never was built on the foundation of God. Isaiah 61:2-3 (Holman Christian Standard) "…to comfort all who mourn, to provide for those who mourn in Zion; to give them a crown of beauty instead of ashes, festive oil instead of mourning, and splendid clothes instead of despair. And they will be called righteous trees, planted by the Lord, to glorify Him." He brought those ashes together in a pile and was beginning to form beauty from them, though it would take us years to see.

Chapter 9

I stood in line in the lobby of this cold, concrete dorm that was to be my home while in college. Girls laughed eagerly around me, while I stood as close as possible to my older, wiser sister. I knew no one in that room but her. Jealousy and self pity ran through my mind as I saw girls with their color-coordinated bedspreads and desk lamps. They had shopped together and probably had already drawn out the layout of how their dorm rooms would be set up. I guess that was easy when you came to college with your best friend, but here I was, eyes darting around the room for a lonely, anxious face such as mine.

"You wanna be my roommate?" I stammered as my sister elbowed me towards a tall, athletic blonde. (Yeah, we would have a lot in common. We could run together in the mornings and then do a few ab crunches at night. Not gonna happen.)

"Sure," she said.

That was it. Immediate friendship, right? This must be what a mail-order bride felt like. Although I now had a roomie, I wasn't at ease with getting to know the sleeping patterns of a girl who was at that college on a cross-country running scholarship. (Again, notice the irony?) And to beat it all, she wasn't going to need me like I needed her. Her boyfriend would be living a few dorms away, also there on the same scholarship.

That evening after setting up my half of my room beautifully with inspirational posters and hues of purple and fuchsia, it was time for my family and my boyfriend to make the two-hour trip back home. After I said my goodbyes by the car to Jason, Mama, and Daddy, my sister agreed to walk me back inside to my room.

"You can do this, Nia," Valerie encouraged me.

"I know, I know. I'll be ok." Who was I convincing? Not myself. She hugged me, and I shut that heavy wooden door, turned the lock, and slid down that door and cried my eyes out. I was alone and needed to be strong. My roommate was probably out running with her boyfriend; our two suite mates, who were best friends from high school, were probably out buying cigarettes and groceries together, and I didn't have a single person.

I decided to busy myself with taking a shower and getting ready for bed. After all, I couldn't be crying in a heap on the floor when all my roommates came back only to have to step over me! As I pulled back the curtain after showering, there, waiting to greet me, was the largest cockroach I've ever seen in my life. If cockroaches have been alive for thousands of years, this must have been the Abraham of roaches; he was the father of them all. I ended his life. It was his time. I did it with one of the suitemates shoes. (What, you thought I'd get its guts on one of my shoes?) It squirted everywhere. Great, now I was lonely and sick to my stomach.

It didn't take long for the loneliness to begin to wear on me. I ate alone, went to the grocery store alone, and attended campus events alone. Most phone conversations with my mother were spent crying and begging to come back home.

"Baby, there's nothing for you here," she would say. "People will be waiting for you to fail and to say that you couldn't make it away at college. You have to stick with your education. It is your only ticket to a better life." My mother and father knew that advice to be so true. Both only received a high school diploma. My father had failed a grade in school and had confessed that to me one day while we sat on the yard swing together.

"Nia, it broke my heart when my class went on ahead of me and left me behind. I always want you to put your grades first and never experience the embarrassment I felt," he had told me.

It didn't matter to me that my heart was breaking there at college. I HAD to stay there for my family and for their honor. I would not allow anyone to get an "I told you so" in on me. Although I believed that I was the one who was controlling my staying or leaving college, I was there for a greater reason, and I wasn't even aware of any behind-the-scenes action that God might have been up to.

Chapter 10

I worked an on-campus job at the Disability Support Services office. The office brailed tests for blind or vision-impaired students, provided classroom interpreters for deaf students, and worked with the professors to ensure students with disabilities were properly accommodated. I not only worked there, I also received services from there. Disability Support Services helped me get a handicapped parking place in front of my dorm.

Because of my loneliness, I was desperate to find friends. That job allowed me to meet friends who were blind. To my surprise, these girls happened to live right across the hall from me in the dorm! Finally, some friends! One girl lived with her seeing-eye dog; another lived with her sister. We would all pile up in my two-door car; the dog would hop in the back with his butt in the seat and his front paws in the floorboard. It was quite a sight (no pun intended) as the wobbly-legged girl helped lead around these blind friends while trying not to trip over the dog.

I believed these relationships were meant to teach me something. At this point in my life, I felt alone in the world while in the college crowd, but I also had, up until this point, felt alone in my disability.

Although I had worked through the awkwardness of being "different" in high school, now I needed to understand the importance of perspective. I admitted that in the past I had wallowed in "Why me?" moments. I had felt that no one else in the world could possibly understand how I felt. In essence, I had ostracized myself when it came to my disease. I didn't allow anyone "in" to that part of my world. I never discussed it, as I surely didn't want to bring any attention to the disease unless someone else asked. These new friends I'd found knew nothing about my difference unless I decided to tell them. They were blind, remember? I could limp around with no stares or questioning glances. But this was a different situation. I WANTED to tell them. I wanted them to know that I understood, in many ways, what it felt like to be "different." There was no threat of an awkward silence after I revealed my disease to them. We simply compared notes.

"Do you know when someone is staring at you?" I asked my blind friends.

"Yes, it's the same feeling as knowing someone has walked into a room while you have your back to the door. You just know they are there. We just feel like someone's staring," they explained.

In the six years since I had been diagnosed with Muscular Dystrophy, I'd spent too much time focusing on how the world had been cruel to me. These girls weren't bitter, and they had every right to be. So what that I could never whistle or wink? They would never know the joy of seeing a smile on a loved one's face. Who cared that I couldn't raise my arms above my head? They would never have a need to raise a hand to block an aggravating sun from their eyes while trying to drive. Why was I focusing on my legs never being able to run again? At least my legs would lead me across a busy crosswalk while my eyes worked to keep me safe from oncoming traffic. They didn't have that luxury. I had much to be thankful for.

Instead, I was blind to what I had been given. They taught me to see what I was capable of rather than focusing on the few hindrances I faced each day. More importantly than what they taught me about my attitude toward my physical setbacks, those two blind girls, the dog, and the sister were about to lead me to a place where my eyes would be open to The Light...

Chapter 11

As we walked into the building of a Christian student organization, I was uneasy. Yes, I knew I was a child of the King, and yes, I had been going to church a little with my sister at home, but *I* knew nothing of Him as my Father. What if they asked me questions about the Bible? Wait, I didn't even own a Bible. But the lure of home-cooked spaghetti during Wednesday's Agape meal and the enticement of silly games with other humans were too much for my lonesome heart to refuse just because of a few fears I had.

Thank God for an overhead projector. During praise and worship meetings, the praise leader would cast the words of songs onto the screen. Now I felt like I had "Amazing Grace" licked because my grandmother had sung it to me as a child, but I wouldn't have known a traditional hymn from a contemporary worship song if they would've flashed up "Traditional" or "Contemporary" on the screen before the songs began. It wasn't relevant. The words mattered, and I could hide my lack of knowledge while reading those words in my mind and singing them from my heart:

"Lord, I lift your name on high.

Lord, I love to sing your praises.

I'm so glad you're in my life.

I'm so glad you came to save us.

You came from heaven to earth to show the way.

From the earth to the cross, my debt to pay.

From the cross to the grave, from the grave to the sky,

Lord, I lift your name on high" (Rick Founds).

They taught us the hand motions, and my weak arms attempted to stay strong enough to convey the cross, grave, and sky, but all I wanted to do was stand there with my face upturned toward heaven. My electric blanket was back, and I was standing in His warmth. My soul ached to sing to Him; tears streamed down my face, as I knew that my body was meant to praise Him, and I had been depriving myself. For the first time ever, *I* wanted the Lord. *I* wanted to know more about His promises. *I* yearned to read and understand His word. I begged Him to stay close to me, so that I could always feel Him. I had turned my back on Him the very day after I had gotten saved when I was fifteen years old and believed this new Christian life was going to be too hard to attempt because I had already messed up by cussing. Although I had gone back on my promise to live for Him, God had kept His promise to me: "I will never leave you nor forsake you"—Hebrews 13:5.

I went to the Christian student organization for weeks without a Bible. I was so embarrassed not to have one of my own, but I so desperately wanted to fall in love with His word. I sucked up my pride and asked one of my suitemates if I could use hers when I went. She was sweet about letting me; however, I always felt like I was wearing a shoe that didn't fit. I had told my sister of the awkwardness of using someone else's Bible, and in September, for my eighteenth birthday, my sister gave me a Bible. A maroon, leather-bound King

James Version with "Nia Cox" imprinted in gold on the front cover. On the first page, she had written, "Trust that the Lord will take care of you"—Psalm 27:14. I was in business; I felt like I was a real-deal Christian now.

One weekend while I was home from college, Valerie's church had a guest preacher. He had lost one of his legs in a vehicle accident. "Good, a guy I can relate to and keep up with in a foot race," I thought. As he preached that night, I knew that I wanted to publicly profess what God had done three years ago in my life and how He was "watering my seed" in the last couple of months through coming to church with Valerie and attending the Christian student organization while at college. During the invitation that night, I went to the altar. (Well actually, it was the stage because there were no spots open at the altar.) It was the first time I had had the nerve to go to the altar, and boy, did it feel good. I tucked my knees beneath me and lay on my face on that stage. I cried until the carpet beneath me was soaked. I begged God to forgive me for how I'd walked away from Him years ago, and I told Him that I was ready to be serious about giving myself over to Him. I rededicated my life to God. (And who had guided me back to the Lord? It was a preacher who had one leg…again, not just a coincidence.)

Now this may all seem a little redundant to you. "Hasn't she already done this?" you may be thinking. I needed to officially reconnect myself with God through Jesus, my Savior and *now* my Lord. It was a turning point for me. It was finally a time that I would allow myself to begin being led by the Holy Spirit, although you will soon see that I still battled flesh. Rededicating my life that night would prove to be the first of many dedications. Actually, I believe every day should be a rededication. Luke 9:23 (New International Version): "Then He said to them all: 'Whoever wants to be my disciple must deny themselves and take up their cross daily and follow me.'" Daily, it said. From the first day I was saved until today as I'm writing this, I have messed up as a Christian. I aim for Christ's target, and I miss the mark every time. I've worn myself out in the past attempting to be better than this flesh will allow. However, there is a freedom that came when I realized, as my pastor loves to say, "Jesus was perfect, so I wouldn't have to be." There is never a demand for us to be perfect. If we could've achieved perfection and complete righteousness, Jesus wouldn't have had to die as a spotless lamb. There is rest that came with the realization that I can be still and let God work out the imperfections inside of me. On that night, on the floor of that stage, I changed. I can't explain it, and I'll never comprehend the mystery of it all, but I rose up off that floor, was baptized in the weeks that followed, and now began to let the world know what the Lord has done for me.

Chapter 12

$\mathcal{E}$verything I was finding out about the Lord through reading His Word and going to church was like putting on a coat after the first cold day of fall, reaching in the pocket, and finding a five dollar bill. Excitement and potential came wrapped up in His promises.

I remember reading Matthew for the first time. (When I had rededicated my life, they gave me an easy-to-understand New Testament.) Well, Matthew was so good, I just had to go on to Mark, then Luke...

"Wait a minute," I thought. "Something's fishy here. They're all telling the same stories, just with different words." Sounds silly and childish, sure, but as a child in the faith, I had so much to learn and had started late, as I was now eighteen.

I began to drive to and from college with the peace of God protecting me, and somehow, I did not feel as lonely. Sure, I still wanted friends to go out to eat with, but I got the vibe I was not alone.

Soon my reactions to stares while I was walking began to change as I thought, "They just don't understand. They stare because they don't know what's wrong. It doesn't always mean they are making fun of me." Little by little, I began to open up to people in my classes. I became light-hearted about my disease and even joked around about it.

"I'm going to run out to the car and get those papers," I might say. My sister would reply, "Well, now if you are going to run, let me go watch. It is a miracle." People did not always know how to take our sick sense of humor, but it was my disease, and I had to laugh about it to keep from crying!

I began to ask God for examples of His presence. I don't know why, then, that I would be amazed when I saw a rainbow or when a conversation with a stranger would turn to how the Lord had chosen me to bestow this disease upon. I began to think of Muscular Dystrophy as "My Strongest Weakness" because the Lord had said to me in 2 Corinthians 12:9 (New International Version), "'My grace is sufficient for you, for my power is made perfect in weakness.' Therefore I will boast all the more gladly about my weaknesses, so that Christ's power may rest on me." Hey, I was a physical weakling. Arms that could not even stay up long enough to put my hair in a ponytail and legs that were now needing to hold on to someone while walking up stairs were quite perfectly weak. I guess that meant that I had a whole lotta God's power resting on me.

Having a relationship with My Savior was more than I imagined it would be. This salvation I was given was NOT just about the one-way ticket to heaven. Sure, I couldn't wait to run around up there for a few thousand years before I settled down to eat and eat and not gain weight. Yes, I couldn't wait to see others who have lived the good life here on earth and now were seeing everything their faith had promised them. More than anything, though, I looked forward to seeing my Heavenly Father. What would He smell like? How would His feet look? (I have always wondered this because surely

I would be unable to have the strength to look at Him in His holy face.) Would His throne have a reclining footrest? Could I climb in His lap, grab a bowl of "golden" popcorn, and watch the footage of my life together, so I could plainly see all that went on behind the scenes while He was at work in me?

As much as I look forward to seeing my life again on video, I wish that it wouldn't be so filled with mistakes like the ones I was about to make.

Chapter 13

W hile sitting in a biology class one day, I was asked by a sorority girl if I would be interested in joining her sorority. I immediately said "no" because I'd been there, and experienced that already with another sorority who had invited me to a "Getting-to-Know-You Social" and then had only gotten to know my name. I felt like I hadn't belonged there, and so I assumed all sororities were the same. I mean, for Pete's sake, I had even asked one of their members what to wear. Then when I got there in my black pants and sweater, they all had on dresses! Well, I might as well have gotten on all fours and let them stretch their high-heeled feet out across my back. I felt like an ottoman...or worse yet, a doormat.

"Just give it a try, Nia. If it is in God's will, it will work out," this classmate said.

Whaa? Did a sorority girl just mention "God's will"? Well, I did not lightly overlook God's confirming acts in my life, so I decided I would give their "Meet and Greet" a shot. Soon, I felt like I was back in high school, laughing and talking with all my girlfriends about what professors to take and which classes to avoid. This sorority had the highest GPA on campus, and they also offered devotional time together. I was sold.

After the social, I rode the elevator downstairs, walked into my dorm room, and called my mama. In what I'm sure sounded like a chipmunk on acid, I attempted to explain how I felt when I was with those girls and how I would "just die" if they did not offer me an invitation into their sorority. As I was reeling on the phone, I heard cheers approaching my door. I jerked it open and stood there grinning like a 'possum eatin' saw briars at the sea of girls yelling sorority chants. (Southern folks will understand.) They handed me a bag of goodies, some balloons, and an invitation to become part of their sisterhood.

My Phi Mu sisters at Jacksonville State University. (I'm on the front row.)

Immediately, I had a family. The next day I wore my new t-shirt depicting that I belonged with the sisterhood of my sorority. I had plenty of offers to go to lunch. From that point forward, I was surrounded by friends, many of whom quickly became best friends. I learned from them that acceptance comes from first accepting yourself. Yes, I had to explain to them about my Muscular Dystrophy. At times, they had lots of questions. I was patient; they were patient with me. They offered to carry heavy objects and take care of physical tasks I could not, but they never made the disease a big deal. I was just Nia to them. Many of them said that they never even noticed my differences after getting to know me. Here I was, part of a college sorority, and I was fitting in with everyone else.

During my junior year of college, my best friend and her mom helped me find a new Muscular Dystrophy doctor in Birmingham, Alabama. With the meeting of this new doctor came the promise of new research and possibly, a cure. I poured all my hopes into this appointment; it also offered the first opportunity for me to ask people to pray about something. I'd never in my life talked openly about God, and now I was going up to my college professors and saying, "I'd like to ask you to pray about this please..."

One day, I stayed around after my math class. This teacher was a kind, Christian woman who had made me love math. (I mean I hated math before like I hated a mosquito bite on the side of my foot. Aggravating and useless, I believed.)

"Would you mind praying for a doctor's appointment I have coming up tomorrow?" I explained to her. I gave her the name of my disease and the expectations I hoped would be met once I met this Muscular Dystrophy specialist.

"Nia, let's just pray right now," she said as she walked around the side of her desk and grabbed my hands. Right then, a bridge between

teacher and student was built, a gap filled. Other students stopped walking out the door and turned to watch.

"Dear Lord..." she began with such authority that I'm sure I heard the rustling of God's robe as He bent down to listen.

When she finished, I thanked her although I knew my true appreciation didn't come out as clearly as I wanted.

"I'll put it on my calendar, Nia. What time does it start? I want to pray specifically for you at that time," she added.

That night I washed my hair and shaved my legs. (I had a feeling all my weak parts would be examined the next day, and I didn't want those tiny forests on my legs hiding any pertinent information.) In mid-hair shampooing, my roommate and sorority sister (I now lived on the sorority floor of the dorm), came screaming and beating on the restroom door.

"Get out, Nia, get out!" she screamed.

"No! Leave me alone," I answered. "I have soap all over my head!"

"You have to get out now," she demanded.

Great, I thought. Now, I'd also need to go to an optometrist tomorrow because I would be blinded by the shampoo that was dripping down my forehead. I jerked open the bathroom door to see my room filled with sorority sisters, and behind them, my dorm room was covered in fluorescent-colored poster paper declaring their hopes, their wishes, and their inspiration for me and my appointment the following day. I knew then, after crying the soap out of my eyes, that the line of the Michael W. Smith song we sang together during sorority recruitment was true: "A friend's a friend forever, if the Lord's the Lord of them." They circled around me and began to pray, lifting their weak and anxious friend to the peace that comes from being in His presence.

I hate to be Negative Nancy here in the midst of this love fest, but something painfully pertinent also happened during this wait for the appointment. *I had one sorority sister come to me for a "private meeting" in my room before I left for Birmingham.*

"Nia," she said. "I just don't believe you are meant to have to live with this disease. Why would God want you to suffer? Forget this appointment, let's just pray right now that God would heal you from this affliction."

Now remember, I was a baby Christian. This girl had grown up in church. She knew so much more than I could ever imagine, so I thought. That night I prayed my guts out that the next morning I would wake up and be healed. I could cancel the appointment and just begin running around campus, telling everyone how the Lord had healed me. When God did not heal me, it sent me into a whirlwind of doubt that lasted for years. I believed that I did not have enough faith to be healed; that I had done something wrong to deserve Muscular Dystrophy. God showed me differently in His word:

"As he went along, he saw a man blind from birth. His disciples asked him, 'Rabbi, who sinned, this man or his parents, that he was born blind?'

'Neither this man nor his parents sinned,' said Jesus, 'but this happened so that the works of God might be displayed in him'" (John 9:1-3, New International Version).

God could heal me if He wanted to. I mean, after all, He was the Creator of the Universe. He knew the ins and outs of this disease. His mighty hands did not slip when He was forming me. "Whoops, I messed up on that chromosome." No, not my God. He just might not WANT to heal me YET. Would the work of God be better displayed in me if I were hobbling or walking straight? I chose the Truth of His word over the opinion of a college girl.

The next day at the appointment, I sat with shaky hands, attempting to fill out that mountain of paperwork that comes when you're a new patient.

"*Well, look who it is!*" *I heard someone say.*

I looked up and was shocked to see none other than my teacher there. The same lady who had prayed with me in her classroom the day before had taken off work to come and sit with my sister and me while we waited for that doctor's appointment. She didn't just show up for that trip but also came back with us a second time for a painful test. I was in college to become a high school teacher. She became my role model at that moment. I, too, wanted to become a teacher who went above and beyond the classroom for my students.

Nothing came of the doctor's appointment, really. No new chance at a cure, no magic medicine. But I realized that God's purpose had been for me to realize that He was constantly surrounding me with people who loved me as I was and who shared in the dream of a future with stronger legs. Maybe there was something about this disease that drew people to me—and maybe, just maybe, my job was to point them back to God as the blind man in the story had done.

Chapter 14

*N*ow fitting in at college, unfortunately, didn't always mean taking part in what I needed to do. With that time in my life came an open opportunity to drink alcohol without my parents' knowledge. In high school I would not have dared to attempt drinking. My mother was always waiting up for me whether I was coming home from a date or the prom. "Come talk to me," she would say. Now my mother was always concerned with what was going on in my life, but don't think she was staying up to chat like best girlfriends. My mother was sniffing me down like a bloodhound. Her nose could detect fingernail polish remover (which I wasn't allowed to use in the house because she had an allergic reaction to it), and it would have easily honed in on alcohol had there ever been any on my breath. I had never seen my parents drink one drop, and if they had learned that I had drunk in college, my body, I'm sure, would have been beaten beyond recognition. (In a loving way, of course, not in a Department of Child Services way.)

I wish that I didn't even have to include this part, but as I'm sure it will be in my movie "It's a Disobedient Life" when I get to heaven, I might as well be honest about it now. It is part of my sin, so there is redemption on the other side of this story! I did drink while in college. I did not even enjoy it. I hated the taste of it, but Thursday nights were our nights to "go out," and I loved being with my girlfriends. I wish that I would have shared the same discipline as the group of girls who were strong in their convictions because I just knew that they would never be caught drinking. Sometimes, I could cover up my dislike of the taste by volunteering to be the designated driver or saying I had to stay back at the dorm to study. Most of the time though, I was too weak. That's what happens when baby Christians put themselves in tempting situations.

I couldn't make it any more in the college world as a young Christian. I would never have dropped out, but I was so tired of coming home on the weekend and throwing myself on the altar to beg for forgiveness. Then, I would drive back to school on Sunday nights, only to walk back into my dorm, cussing and making plans for Thursday night. Oh, I felt horrible the whole time. I was sick of the double life. I wanted the Lord, and I wanted a righteous life, but I just couldn't withstand the temptations that faced me when I drove back into my college town. I am ashamed. I am thankful I did not have to live in that shame for long…

I Corinthians 10:13 states that "No temptation has overtaken you except what is common to mankind. And God is faithful; He will not let you be tempted beyond what you can bear. But when you are tempted, He will also provide a way out so that you can endure it." My way out was to get out of college soon. I took twenty-one hours of classes one semester. I signed up for summer courses. I was determined to finish in three and a half years because that was one less semester of separating myself from the presence of the Lord by continuing to live in this sin.

One May mini-mester, I ran into a dilemma. I could not continue to live in the dorm for that month. I knew I did not have enough money nor could I get an apartment. Actually, I did not even have the money to take the classes that month. God works through others. At a family function, He must have told my uncle to pass me an envelope with six hundred dollars in it. (Just enough for the two classes' tuition.) God also pricked the heart of that same sweet math teacher who had shown up at my doctor's appointment: she asked me if I would like to come and live with her and her husband for a month. (Can you believe this woman?)

She and her husband could not have children of their own, so their house felt fairly empty to them, and their guest room was wide open. Her husband was a locksmith who loved to watch *The Andy Griffith Show*, and she offered nighttime advice in the kitchen after supper. That month was short; classes were fast-paced; but the lesson was stamped into my heart: "Give more than is required as a teacher, as a person, as a Christian."

(By the way, years later, this sweet couple was able to have a child of their own. Although I cannot begin to think as God thinks, I would like to believe that they were given a child of their own in return for their obedience to take in a child of God's own.)

Chapter 15

A s my time at college neared an end, so began my future as a high school teacher. I was eager to begin my practicum teaching, which comes before student teaching. (Practicum teaching allows you to go into a school and observe and teach a couple of lessons a week. Student teaching requires you to fulfill all responsibilities a full-time teacher would as you are there learning under a supervising veteran educator daily.) However, my teaching career would have a few more concerns and questions than a typical "newbie" would encounter. "What if they make fun of my walking? What if they are disrespectful? What if I cannot keep up with them while they are coming back from the lunchroom?" A million thoughts ran through my mind as I took the podium at my practicum school for the first time.

I laid it all out on the line. "Hello, my name is Miss Cox. I have Muscular Dystrophy. It is a disease that weakens my muscles as I get older, but you don't need to be worried that it is contagious because it can't get on you!"

As I bared my faults, their pencils dropped. Slowly their heads raised and their eyes diverted from their doodling. I had them right where I wanted them. Those seniors changed from the cold-hearted response of, "Great, here comes another one of these wannabe teachers to experiment on us" to a kind-eyed "Wow, she just told us something that was wrong with her. Maybe I can tell her something that is wrong with my life."

I drove back to my dorm room that day on Cloud 9,000. I screamed. I praised the Lord. I even took my hands off the wheel and drove with my knee, so I could try to raise my feeble arms to heaven in praise. (I also think that God kept me from passing any police officers as I was attempting to praise Him!) I knew that the decision I had made to change from majoring in Marine Biology, to pharmacy, to secondary education was the right one. It was a confirmation from the Lord and a kick in the butt to hurry up, get out of college, get home, and get a teaching job. There were students out there who did not know they needed me. Plus, there was a red-headed electrician named Jason who had stayed true to me while I got my education, and we had spent too many weekends driving home to see each other. I was ready to see him all the time. I was eager to get married; thank God He gives men a brain to think with instead of their hearts. Jason wanted to wait until we were financially ready, and I thought we could "live off love." I looked at rings constantly and, if you could call Hiroshima a hint, well, that's how big I dropped 'em.

As I so often have, I was rushing life and ordering events to happen in *my* time, not the Lord's. But God knows best. He always does. Although I was about to severely doubt it.

Chapter 16

$\mathcal{I}$ graduated magna cum laude (or as my pastor says, "Thank you, Lordy") in December of 2001 and in January started working on my Master's degree while being blessed to fill a maternity leave position at a school for a few months. I mean, who even finds a teaching job in the spring? It was nice to have the Lord watching out for you.

Living at home allowed me to, once again, rededicate myself to living for God. I was able to focus on falling in love with Him, and that meant knowing how to conduct myself in a way that showed my love.

Now, this proved a rocky time for Jason and me. Jason was still working construction out on the road, and he was battling with drinking himself. I would not say that he ever had a "problem," but he enjoyed having a beer, which led to several, each night after work. We also faced a sin in our personal relationship. I had become convicted about this area of my life and had thus told Jason I wanted to listen to what God was telling me about it. But as I became closer to the Lord, Jason and I grew apart. He was not experiencing these same convictions and all he knew was that the girl he had fallen in love with was changing and the way it made him feel was guilty. He still held the same aversion to church as he did when he was younger. Remember that he had been made to go to church all his life, so he was not eager to go with me although I was always raving about how much I loved my church and my pastor.

I remember calling him one Sunday morning.

"Are you going to come to church with me today?" I said.

"Probably not," he simply stated.

"After all God has done for you in one week, do you not think that you could give Him one day of worship?" I demanded.

Sounded smart right? Yeah, and very holier than thou. I'm sure you're shocked that I did not win one for the God team that day. (I have since learned in Proverbs 25:24 [The Message] that it is "Better to live alone in a tumbledown shack than share a mansion with a nagging spouse." I probably had him ready to jump off the edge of the house, and we weren't even married yet, nor in the same house!)

That day at church, I went to the altar. My older male cousin, whose godly marriage I admired, came and helped me lift my boyfriend of six years to the Lord. I left that worry and care there at God's feet. It was too heavy for me to bear, and I loved Jason too much to mess it up with my Jr. Holy Spirit attitude.

By this time in my life, my mother and father had also started coming to church. There we all were. With cousins and aunts and uncles together, we took up the first three pews on the front right side of the church. We were the loud "Amen" corner, quick to clap along with songs and quick to cry. I had a feeling that we were a little more vocal than this church (the one my parents had formerly left) was used to hearing. We could not help it. We had a lot to praise God for. I loved the peace that came with knowing we were all here worshipping together, and I wanted Jason to be a part of it because I wanted my future marriage to be founded on The Rock.

1 PETER 3:1-2 (New International Version) "Wives, in the same way be submissive to your husbands so that, if any of them do not believe the word, they may be won over without words by the behavior of their wives, when they see the purity and reverence of your lives." This verse came true for me before I became a wife. I learned to keep my mouth shut. Yes, I was dying every time he didn't walk through those church doors on a Sunday morning. Yes, I felt like Jason was missing out on so much that I was learning about. Yes, I was terrified that my marriage that had not even begun yet would end like my sister's had if God was not at the center of it.

One Sunday Jason came. "No, now don't push it, Nia," I told myself. "Do not try to force Sunday School on him too. One step at a time." His shyness was hard to overcome during greeting time. He mostly stood there with his arms down to his side while strangers welcomed him. On the first Sunday in December, he did not come for fear that he would have to walk to the front with all the other birthday and anniversary celebrators. At least Jason was there all the other times. God would take care of the rest. It would be mysteriously, that's for sure, but God would change Jason in His own way.

Chapter 17

*T*here we all were in the church pew. Packed in like sardines, my whole family, together, allowing the truths of God's sustaining grace to penetrate our hearts. We would soon need that lesson...

In the spring of 2002, my daddy started coughing. It was a rattling cough deep in his chest that would prove more than bronchitis. He had lung cancer. The day my mom and dad found out, I was at Jason's family's house. While sitting in the living room, his grandmother handed me the phone. I expected my parents to tell me that it was time to come home, but instead, my mother told me that his tests had come back positive for cancer. I do not remember how the phone got back into his grandmother's hand, but in the next second, I was pushing my face deep into his mother's toilet, attempting to purge the information that had just entered my body. If I heaved hard enough, I couldn't hear the thoughts screaming in my head: "Oh God, not my daddy! Oh God, not my daddy!" Past images flashed across my eyes: him picking me up by the tiny gallowses of my overalls that matched his as he threw me up into the cab of his '66 Chevy; Daddy coming into my room at night to rub out the cramps in my aching, weak legs;

his thundering laugh, which caused his whole body to shake up and down; the cautious rustling of a butterscotch candy bag in the living room because my mama didn't need to know my diabetic father had any hidden. What if all these images became memories? I was overwhelmed with the idea of life without my daddy. I didn't want to raise my head out of that toilet bowl because at least what I could see was contained in one ivory porcelain area. Jason came along behind me and held my hair. He told me it was going to be alright, but I knew it was not going to be.

That night when I went home, many of our relatives were there. I wanted to scream, "He's not dead! Why are you bringing food? Why are we in here talking about him while he sits in the living room and watches Westerns?"

Daddy wasn't taking the news so well himself. His opinion that night at supper was, "Oh well, why not eat what I want to eat? I'm gonna die anyway." I was angry at him for not wanting to fight, and it reminded me again how not choosing to fight my own disease would affect those who loved me. Never does sin only impact the sinner. Everyone around gets caught in the ripple effect of the sinking stone of sin. That night at the dinner table, the sin was doubt.

God was good to us. Lamentations 3:22-23 (New International Version) promises, "Because of the LORD's great love we are not consumed, for His compassions never fail. They are new every morning; great is your faithfulness."

The next morning, we awoke with hope. I cannot explain how that implantation had happened in our brains during the night, but it was there the following day. Radiation was given to my daddy for several months, and it was successful and not as painful as chemotherapy, we had heard. The Lord had spared us, and we were back on the mountaintop again, still sitting in the church pews together, still raising our hands in praise and being even louder in church. Hey, we had even more to be thankful for.

Chapter 18

J ason proposed unexpectedly to me in December of 2002.
In my sorority, we had a tradition called a "candle lighting."
Typically, after a sister got engaged, she would tell a close friend
who would decorate a candle to bring to a chapter meeting. After the
meeting, we would gather around, turn off the lights, sing a song, and
pass this candle around. No one (but the person who had made the
candle) would know who had gotten engaged. When we came to the
part of the song that said, "engagement," the friend who had made the
candle would step across the circle to the girl who had become engaged.
The blushing new bride-to-be would blow the candle out and proceed
to tell everyone the story of how her fiancé proposed. Now, I had sat
through a blue million of these ceremonies while I was in college. It was
all I could do to keep from rolling my eyeballs when yet another girl who
had dated her beau for two months got engaged, when, at this point, I
had dated Jason Stivers for six years.

So on this particular day, I had planned to attend a sorority sister's
wedding. I had asked Valerie to go with me, and for some strange reason,
Jason was eager to go along. I had not even asked him. I did not believe
he would want to spend his Saturday at a wedding. Valerie was along

for companionship as well as a spy. She had her video camera because I knew that whenever my time came, I wanted to have a Christmas-themed wedding. She was going to be videoing the decorative ideas.

During the reception of a sorority sister's wedding, we all circle around the bride, sing the same song as the candle light ceremony, and then one of the sisters steps out with the candle and allows the bride to blow out the candle when the song says "marriage." We had just finished standing around the bride, when one of my sorority sisters whispered to me, "Nia, you are not going to believe it. Jane Doe is going to get engaged tonight. She does not know it, but her boyfriend is going to step out during another candle lighting and propose!"

We made our way out of the reception area and into a hallway where this "surprise" candle lighting was going to take place.

"Oh, Jane Doe," I thought. "How exciting! You have no idea. Wait, where is your boyfriend? He didn't even come with you tonight. Maybe he is going to burst through the doors at the word 'engagement'! How romantic!"

I was so focused on singing the words of the song, trying not to look Jane Doe in the eye, and attempting not to grin, that I was shocked when my "big sister" in the sorority stepped across the circle and she, along with the candle, were standing in front of me!

"What's going on?" I thought.

My friend shook her head "yes" indicating that, indeed, my time had come.

I started bawling and lay over on my friend. It is a miracle in itself that all that mousse I had in my curly black fro did not catch on fire as I propped on her and wept.

Softly behind me, I felt a little jerk, jerk, jerk on the bottom of my sweater. I turned to see Jason, my red-headed sweetie petie, on one knee with my dream ring glistening out of its box.

"Nia, will you marry me?" he stammered.

Who could answer? I transferred my weight from my friend to Jason's shoulder and now proceeded to lay over on him and soak his shirt.

"Did she say 'yes'?" someone asked.

"I don't know yet," Jason replied. (Like there was a question as to what I would say!)

I nodded while my head was still on his shoulder. It was all I could do. I was broken down. And to beat it all, there was my sister with me, videoing it all!

I broke into the ugly cry after Jason's romantic proposal.

That was a positive way to end 2002, as I had also received my first teaching job (where I presently work.) Now I was all abuzz with making wedding plans for December of 2003. But it wasn't long into 2003 that I started enduring a pain in my stomach that felt like constant menstrual cramps. After a series of tests and ultrasounds, the doctor said I needed laparoscopic surgery to remove some endometriosis the size of a pool ball from my uterus. The doctor felt that my pain would be over and that I would be on the mend. I did not have time to remember what it was like to live without pain because the pain in my stomach was replaced by pain in my heart. It was a year later than the first time, and Daddy's cancer was back.

Chapter 19

One Friday afternoon in February, a nurse from our family doctor called.

"Miss Cox, we would like to schedule a time on Monday for your family to come in and go over the test results."

"Monday? You want us to wait until Monday? You are looking at the test results, yet you want us to wait an entire weekend to see if my daddy's cancer is back or not? Tell me the results now," I demanded.

"Ma'am, I'm sorry," she said. "With the new insurance privacy policies, we are unable to disclose that information over the phone."

"Then do not call on a Friday evening!" I screamed. "Can you imagine what this is like waiting to know if your father's cancer is back or not?" Suddenly, the doctor's voice was on the phone, calming me down, and reminding me that it was not the nurse's fault.

I was not angry at her anyway. I was angry at cancer. I knew it had raised its ugly head again the second I heard his racking cough coming from the living room one night. I wanted to punch cancer. I wanted to rip it to pieces and make it feel the pain it had inflicted on my family.

Monday's results were positive, as we had suspected. We readied ourselves in our roller coaster seats, strapped down our harnesses, and white-knuckled the next few months of chemotherapy. If radiation had been Popeye, chemotherapy was Rocky Balboa to my daddy's insides. He was so sick during this time, but we trusted in the Lord, and again, He proved Himself still in the miracle-working business.

I was back at college for the summer, living with a sorority sister, and preparing to finish my Masters degree along with my much dreaded comprehensive exams. My mother called my cell phone one day while I was working on one of two research papers that were due. "Nia, your daddy's cancer is gone! The doctors said it would just take about a month for him to get the chemotherapy out of his body before he'll begin to feel good again. Praise God! It is over!"

Her phone call had come on a Saturday. My sister's phone call came the following Wednesday. "Nia, you need to get your comprehensive exams moved up from Saturday to as soon as you can. Daddy's in the hospital. He has too many complications from the chemo in reaction with his diabetes, failed knee replacements, etc. You need to come home."

I immediately went to work talking to my professors to get my exams moved up. I went into a classroom on Friday, and four hours later, I was sitting in my car, looking down at my cell phone, and dreading to call my sister's number. I knew that she had been withholding news until I got finished with my exams so that I could concentrate on studying.

"Tell me the truth, Valerie. What's going on?" I asked.

"He doesn't have much time, Nia," she answered. "You need to come home fast."

I know that it does not seem fair after all that I have described to you that the Lord had done for us, but when I received that news, I could have cared less about talking to God. Yet, He was still providing for me. Jason, was, for the first time, on a construction job in Alabama. Not only that, the job was only thirty minutes away from my college. I called him and begged him to come drive me home.

As I walked into my friend's apartment to wait for Jason, I dropped to the floor. I screamed at the top of my lungs. I pulled at my hair. My temples were soaked from tears rolling back into my hair line. "Why God? We begged You to let him live! God, I'm supposed to get married in five months. Why would you take him away now? He'll never be able to walk me down the aisle!" Then, the prayers/screams stopped. I could not and did not want to talk to God again. I was angry with Him, He had not shown up for me, and I had nothing else to say. Later, I learned that there was prayer going on despite my angry mouth not moving: Romans 8:26 (New International Version) "In the same way, the Spirit helps us in our weakness. We do not know what we ought to pray for, but the Spirit himself intercedes for us with groans that words cannot express."

I heard Jason come to the apartment door. I could not get up to answer. He softly opened the door and found me lying on the floor. He picked me up, placed me on the bed, and began to rock my shoes onto my feet. His tender hand cupped behind my neck, pulled me to him off the bed, and set me on my feet. He kept one hand on me, lest I fall over, while he reached into the bathroom to get an entire roll of toilet paper to take with us on the trip. He's always been able to think one step ahead of what I think I need. We got into the car, I curled into the fetal position with the entire roll of toilet paper shoved under my nose, and we drove. I mean we drove, with hazard lights on, we drove.

The weekend with Daddy was spent right by his side at the hospital. I felt I could not get close enough to him. I climbed into the bed beside him and listened to him breathe. I felt his furry warmth:

There were those leg hairs I used to play "beauty shop" with as I would cut them with childproof scissors while holding a tissue beneath the falling hairs. Here was that hairy mass of chest that had been naked when he came to the middle school dance to pick me up in just some cotton shorts and his house shoes. (I had run out of that dance in embarrassment.) Beside me were those black-haired arms whose strength had once flipped me up onto his shoulders, so that I could see the world from a six-foot-six view. Now those arms didn't seem as muscular and the flesh hung loosely on their frame. That first evening, I just needed to lie by him. There were no words. I just had to feel the reality of his body, rising and falling with his breath, breath that I didn't want to leave.

That night, back at home, I slept with mama. I was on Daddy's side of the bed. I remembered that when Daddy had worked night shift and was not around at bedtime, I would go into their bedroom and kiss Mama good night and then kiss Daddy's pillow. That way, his kiss would be waiting for him when he got in from work. Now my head was resting where his head should have been home sleeping.

My voice broke the darkness of their bedroom, "Mama, do you think it's weird that I want to go and get my wedding dress out of the bridal shop and take it to the hospital to put on for Daddy tomorrow?"

"I don't think that would be strange at all, baby," she replied.

So the next morning I drove to the bridal shop and got my wedding dress. I thought about how strange it was that the first time I would wear my wedding dress would be in a hospital. When I got there, I went into the stark white bathroom, moved over the urine measuring pans, and proceeded to delicately place myself into my dream wedding gown. I looked at the mirror at my unruly curly hair and decided to put it into a ball with a hair tie I had around my wrist. I slipped my glistening tiara over that tuft of hair and laid flat the veil which hung down my back. I sweated nervously because I wanted Daddy to think I looked beautiful. My sweaty hands turned the knob of the bathroom door into a hospital room where my mother, sister, and a visiting couple from church waited. (Wouldn't you know that they just happened to have a camera with them so we could keep a record of this moment?) I stepped out onto the slick tile of the room in just my sock feet. My daddy was sitting on the edge of the bed, looking at me.

"Oh baby," he said. "Oh baby. You are beautiful. I am so proud of you." I rushed to him and cried as we spread the train of my dress out across the bed to take pictures. It was our immobile walk down the aisle. Impending death had not stolen my moment. I still got to have that father reaction to seeing his daughter in her wedding dress. I was still getting to hold his hand.

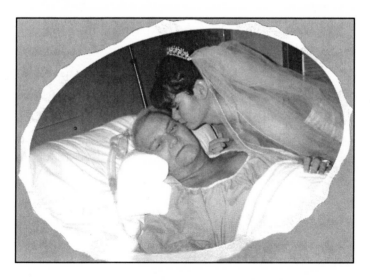

Although I had imagined my father walking me down
the aisle, I would be thankful for these precious final
moments with him in that hospital room.

I dreaded the next day. It was Sunday, and I had to go back to college. I know that seems so unimportant, but I had only days left to finish a program I had been selected for, and if I didn't finish those hours, I would be unable to graduate with my Masters degree at the end of the week. So that evening, as I prepared to tell my father goodbye, I sat on the side of the bed opposite the side he was on. His feet touched the floor on one side; mine dangled like a child's on the other. What words could I say about how I felt toward him? How could I possibly begin to remember all I had planned to say? I began to speak, but could only swallow back my tears.

"Stop that mess," Daddy's still strong voice broke the air.

And so that was what was said. I was glad we were sitting opposite one another. I could lean my head over on his shoulder, and he would still be unable to see my face contort in pain.

"We have to go, Nia." Jason had walked into the room and was preparing to take me back to college. He and Daddy had already had time together that weekend. He had promised Daddy he would take care of me. My daddy loved Jason Stivers, and Jason Stivers loved my daddy. They had also been together six and a half years.

I now was standing facing the head of his bed. "You have to go on back, baby. You have to get your education. You have to finish that degree. I'm so proud of you. Now go on back, and finish this thing," he comforted me. Even in the end, he was still taking care of his baby girl.

As I placed my hand on the doorknob, I turned to see my daddy's face for the last time. I knew I would never see his hazel eyes look at me in pride again. I managed a weak smile; then with all the strength I could muster in my body, I turned and walked out the door.

The very next night, back at the apartment at college, Valerie called.

"It's time, Nia," she said. "He's gone."

That day he had stopped responding to anyone. Valerie had said it had been horrible and that they had wanted to shake him to ask him to talk. All he had said was "Oh, Lord. Oh, Lordy." His eyes were already fixed on the Promised Land and his Savior whom he was hours away from meeting.

I sat up on the bed, looked at three of my sorority sisters who were there in the apartment with me, and gave in when one patted the pillow in her lap. I lay my head down on her and allowed her to rub my hair. The other two sisters petted me while we waited for Jason to arrive to take me home. Not much had to be said, but they were there with me, and their presence helped me face the fears of the days to come.

When Jason picked me up, we headed, hazard lights flashing, to the hospital. I know it may sound stupid because he was already dead, but I wanted to get there fast. I wanted to see him before the funeral home came and picked up his body. My cousin opened my car door when we pulled up at the entrance of the hospital. I lay on her and let her carry my body, feet dragging, to the elevators. Around the corner, down the wing, his body would be waiting. The body I had loved for so long would be in the room, but his soul would be gone.

They left me in the room with him. His mouth was slightly open as were his eyes. Death is not pretty as TV would have you believe. I did not care. I was not scared. I climbed in the bed with that body, my daddy, and I told him all that I had not been able to the day before. Somehow I hoped that his soul was hovering close by, listening. I asked him to send me a sign, to let me know that he was watching over me. I believe that it would be too sad if God allowed our loved ones to see us here on earth in pain and missing them, and I don't believe there are tears or sadness in heaven; however, I do believe that through God, signs can be sent that give us assurance. (To this day, I see red birds often. Red was the color Daddy always said looked best on me. I see red birds most often when I'm praying in the car or thinking of Daddy. One will shoot across the road right in front of my car as if to say "I see you, baby. I'm so proud of you." One morning a whole flock of "Daddy birds" were in our front yard. There are no coincidences with God.)

We buried my father on my parents' thirty-seventh wedding anniversary. We all sat packed in together on the pew of the funeral home. This time, my daddy was missing from our seating section, but one had been added. Yes, after five long years, Valerie had progressed from the heartache of divorce, to the unconditional love of God, to dating men who turned out to be "duds." God had finally, six months earlier, brought her the man who could meet the requirements on the list she had created. She would settle, this time, for no less than a man of God, and now he could be here to take care of her after we lost our first love in life—our daddy. My daddy could also have reassurance, before dying, that both his girls had good men to take care of them. Talk about the timing of God, huh?

As my cousin sang "I Can Only Imagine," I felt my hands rising in praise at the idea of the place that God has prepared for us. My dad's knee was no longer aching. A dry cough would not rise in his chest. At one point during the funeral I thought, "Wait, God. I'm supposed to be mad at you. Why do I feel ok right now?"

Although I deserved no answer, I softly heard a scripture rise back into my memory: "And the peace of God, which surpasses every thought, will guard your hearts and minds in Christ Jesus" (Philippians 4:7, Holman Christian Standard).

Chapter 20

$\mathcal{J}$ ason Stivers changed after my father's death. He simply explained to me that he realized that he needed to step up, quit drinking, and be the man I needed him to be now that he was the only man I had left. Writing that out now makes God's handiwork seem obvious, but for years I had struggled with understanding the untimely death of my father. My testimony had always included, "I may never know why, on this side of heaven, that God took my father five months before my wedding." I was not angry with God anymore, but I simply had come to an understanding that we don't always receive a revelation of what God is up to. But one night, five years after my father's death, I was attempting to help another woman who was aggravated with her son-in-law for not consistently following after God. As I explained to her that Jason had changed when Daddy died, the confirmation from my Savior hit me: had my daddy not died before my wedding, Jason might not have become the husband that God instructs men to be. When all I had focused on was the loss of my father, Jehovah Jireh ("God provides") was giving me the head of the household this bride would need.

Jason and I experienced the wedding of our dreams, or my dream, at least. (Heck, I'd now waited seven years. I had had PLENTY of time to plan out the details!) Everything went smoothly: my father's memory was present; I didn't trip coming down the aisle alone; the slideshow of pictures worked perfectly; no one set themselves ablaze as the congregation lit their candles off our unity candle (they were symbolizing that they would continue to pray for us). I kissed Jason as exactly the right words of Etta James's song "At laassst, my love has come along..." played in the speakers. The entire town seemed to share in our excitement and had come out to support us.

I loved knowing we were married on the stage of the church my family had once left and where God had brought my sister's broken ashes back. It was the stage where I had laid my face prostrate before the Lord and begged His forgiveness. That stage was where our church family had gathered and placed their hands on my father and my family in prayer. We were starting this marriage off not only on this sacred stage but also on a foundation built upon our love for the Lord and how He had changed and would continue to change our lives.

The Lord has made us one...FINALLY!

Chapter 21

After getting married in December, I began to experience pain again in my belly in January. I felt badly all the time. While teaching, I would often have to sit down at my desk and double over in pain. In my life I have come to believe that a hot bath, a nap, or a heating pad can solve almost anything, but this hurt was not going away any time soon. I was sure there was a little man living amongst my ovaries whose sole purpose was to do the Mexican hat dance on them twenty-four hours a day. No, that sounds a little too much like a tickle since there was also a vice grip around them while he danced.

It was back to the doctor for me. More tests and ultrasounds confirmed that the endometriosis was back. (Only one year after we had taken out the pool ball-sized tumor.)

"Nia, one way to get rid of endometriosis is to get pregnant," she advised me. (That was the craziest idea I had ever heard. You would think that getting pregnant would be dangerous when you already had the tiny dancer living in there.)

Pregnancy. Children. Those were issues all their own. When I was eleven, I had been told by the doctor who diagnosed me with

Muscular Dystrophy that if I had children in the future, there would be a fifty/fifty chance that my child would also inherit the disease. So all my life I had fought those odds in my mind. My reasoning was that although Mama had MD, Valerie was not born with it. (This gave me good reason to tease Valerie and tell her that she had sucked all the good genes out of Mama, and I was left with all the bad ones.) My logic was that I could have one child, it would get the strong genes I had to offer, and I would be happy with just one. Made sense, right? Well, I guess that is why I am not a doctor. Years later, when I had met the new MD doctor in Birmingham, she had explained that genetic inheritance didn't quite work the way I had drawn out the little Punnett Square in my mind.

"Muscular Dystrophy is a dominant gene," she described. "Although your husband may be perfectly healthy, your child(ren) will most likely take on the disease. It is like having a brown-eyed father and a blue-eyed mother. Chances are, the child will have brown eyes because it is the dominant trait."

"Hmmpph," I thought. "I'll show her. What does she know? It was dominant in my mother and only one of her children has it. We will just cross that bridge when we get there."

Hello bridge. Now here I was, twenty-three years old, standing hand-in-hand with Jason on one side of a swinging bridge with a possible red-headed baby waiting on the other side.

I left the gynecologist's office that day on a mission to research my odds. The Muscular Dystrophy society on the web was filled with inspirational mothers who pushed the limits and had, at times, been successful at having children who weren't showing signs of the weaknesses. Please do not misunderstand me. It would not be a detriment to have a child with MD; if I believed that, then I would also agree that I should have never been born. However, my mother and I were the only two in my family to have the disease. I know how hard it had been on Mama to see me struggle physically and emotionally along the way. "With every generation, MD shows up earlier and earlier," I had been told. Mama was in her thirties when she was diagnosed—I was eleven. What if my child never experienced running or playing as we had been able to do? It was now my choice to decide if I wanted to continue to pass this genetic monster down through the generations.

In my research, there were also women who were honest enough to say that the strain of carrying a child inside their bodies was enough to make them unable to walk again after child birth. A wheelchair. Great. That was one of my worst fears. My mother was in a wheelchair by this time, and I wanted to fight that presumptuous future like a firefighter fought a flame. I had seen the way that she struggled when we shopped, all the clothes racks staring down at her and grabbing on to the arm of her chair. At town functions, people wanted to pity her, saying, "Now Beatrice, why are you in that chair?"

"Oh, I was worried there wouldn't be any seats, so I brought my own," she would sometimes reply. (Sarcasm was also obviously inherited.)

Although my mother had accepted that a wheelchair offered her freedom versus not being able to go at all, I was not to that noble realization yet. That was not a road I wanted to go down.

I continued to read stories of women who were in labor for hours, mightily trying to birth their children like "normal" women; they had ended up with Cesarean sections because the lack of stomach muscles would not allow them to push hard enough. Many had struggled throughout their pregnancies, not just during the childbirth.

The odds were not in my favor. Passing on dominant genes, becoming wheelchair bound, and experiencing complicated pregnancies were not what I had planned to battle. All my life, I imagined that it was just a choice of having one child and hoping that he or she would not have the disease. This bridge was swinging a little too much, and my legs were feeling more and more unstable for the journey.

But there was another person who would be taking this journey: Jason. Now, you need to know a little about Jason and children. He is one of those people who gets this kind of response from parents regarding their children: "Look at her. She never just takes up with men like that! Look at how she's lying over on his shoulder, patting his back." When we played with baby cousins or church kids, they ran to him. In fact, he would eventually come to teach the four and five-year-old children's Sunday School class. He was a baby stealer from way back. No one else could hold a baby when he was around. I had seen the way he would hold my baby cousin and caress his tiny sausage-link arms with his own work-worn hands.

Children seem to be drawn to my sweet husband.
Here he is giggling with our nephew Cooper.

I, on the other hand, had not been given a maternal bone in my body, I believed. I was scared to hold babies because of their bobble heads. What if my arms were not strong enough to support them? The scent of a poopy diaper made me gag. What if that got on my hand? Walking down the elementary hallway of our kindergarten through twelfth grade school almost made me have an anxiety attack as children would come rushing up to tattle, "Billy just looked at me!" I wanted to say, "And your point is?" (Sarcasm just does not work as well on little ones as it does with high school students, who could understand and appreciate it.) Little kids get in your personal bubble where they proceed to cough and snot all over you. Yeah, I just needed to stick with older kids; they were my comfort zone.

"So maybe I was not meant to be a mother," I told myself. As I was trying to explain that to my head, no one told that to my aching heart.

Jason and I spent many nights lying in bed with our options invisibly painted on the ceiling of the room. In his mind, there were no choices. He simply refused the idea of children if it compromised my health. "It is just not worth it to me," he would say.

I believed he was just being kind. Surely, such a kid magnet would want to see his own little boy or girl bolting into his arms. I was terrified that deep down inside, he resented marrying me. As if Muscular Dystrophy weren't enough, now his wife of one month had endometriosis for a second time. Could he return me? I was a lemon of a wife. Finally, I worked up the nerve to ask him. I was terrified of his answer:

"I want you. I fell in love with you. I am happy with our life being just the two of us. We can hop in the truck and go when we want to go. We can nap when we want to nap. Nothing stops us from what we want to do. I'm ok if it is always just us," he answered.

I did not deserve him. He was another of God's gracious blessings. Although I heard Jason's heartfelt words, I would have tried being

Superwoman and risked carrying a baby inside me if I had thought, for any moment, that he might change his mind about children.

I decided to go to another doctor for a second opinion.

"Nia, I would never advise anyone your age to have a hysterectomy, but with this reoccurrence of your endometriosis and with your dilemma of child-bearing because of your disease, I would tell you that if you wanted to have a hysterectomy, I would understand."

My doctor confirmed his opinion. "We could do another laparoscopic surgery to remove the endometriosis that has formed since last year, but the truth is that we would have to continue to do the surgery over and over. It will just keep coming back."

Although I prayed for guidance in this life-altering decision, it was hard to hear an answer past the pain I was constantly experiencing. I began to feel like I was losing my mind. Feeling badly for so long begins to wear on you mentally. As good as my sweet husband was to me, I was ill with him. Why do we always hurt people that we know will continue to be there for us? Unfortunately, when the pain was ripping my insides apart, I wanted to be quiet, still, and in the fetal position. The feisty girl Jason had married was finding it hard to make it through each day. Teaching was hard that year. I probably missed out on helping kids who might have needed me because all I could focus on was my tender stomach and the ominous choice concerning having a hysterectomy.

We made the decision to have the surgery at the end of the school year. I had never even received confirmation from God on what the answer was; yet we held on to the assurance that our future was in His hands, as it always had been. He would take care of any choices we may face later on, such as to adopt or not. But trusting God is not always as easy as it sounds. I would still have to take many more steps in the darkness of childlessness before I could find the light of God's possibilities.

Chapter 22

*A*fter the hysterectomy, I spiraled into a walking, well-hidden depression. It began with lying on the couch, recovering, and watching one of those stinkin' made-for- hysterical-women TV movies. Wouldn't you know that it was about a couple who had decided to adopt a child from another country? Well, the woman died in some horrible accident, and the man was left to take care of this new child alone. The adoption agency came and took the baby away because then the child's environment was not as it was originally described in the paperwork. The dad fought and fought to get his baby girl back and eventually succeeded. Guess who was squalling her head off?

"I know! I know how you feel!" I yelled at the TV dad. (Thank God Jason was gone to work. He would have changed the channel and said, "Why do you watch this mess anyway? Don't do this to yourself." Who wanted to hear rationale at a time like that?)

When I went back to the gynecologist for a post-op appointment, a couple sat beside me in the waiting room. They had a baby, and he was cute...really cute, and he had red hair. In my mind I played out the scene of stealing him and running to the car. I could proudly bring him home to Jason as a cat brings a prized mouse to the doorstep. The fantasy did not last long. Who could even run out of the office? They would have me tackled and arrested in two seconds. (Please do not think I'm crazy unless you have been there yourself.)

While waiting in the examining room I heard another couple talking through the wall. They were giggling and cooing over one another. Apparently, they were there to figure out if they were pregnant or not. I heard the door open and close. The doctor had walked in. Mumble. Mumble. Squeals. Great. I couldn't escape it. On the other side of that wall, a husband and wife were finding out the most exciting news of their lives, and on my side, I was suffering with having made the decision to rob myself of ever feeling that excitement. I lay my head on that lilac-colored wall, turned my face away from the door, and attempted to muffle my cries with my arm.

By the time the doctor walked in, I had dried it up. I did not want to make her believe that she would have to create a padded, barred room for barren women. My doctor was wonderful to me. She did not refute my feelings of depression. She simply reminded me that I had made the best decision to take care of my body for myself, my husband, and my possible future family.

"Adoption might be an option down the road," she reminded me.

At that point, I could not think of children who were not my own, but it gave me hope. I needed all I could get.

Twenty-one babies were born to my rather small church family that year. I had to force my hands together to clap when couples brought their new babies, bundled in beautiful decorative blankets, to the front of the church to announce their birth, weight, length, and praise to God. I, personally, thought it was cruel to those of us who had no swaddled offering to bring. I would look around the church on Mother's Day, as all the women went to the front to get their Mother's Devotional, at those of us who were left in the pews. There were those who were much older, and there were those who were much younger and were not married yet. I felt alone…again.

I looked for "traveling companions" on this lonely road. I went to women's conferences hoping to hear a lady speak about how she made it through this hurt. I always left feeling full in other areas of my Christian walk, but my womb, or lack thereof, was still empty.

My cousin, who was in high school at the time, had a baby unexpectedly. At church I would hold him and spend the entire service looking down at him. I'm sure my family just thought I was enjoying holding a baby, as most people do. But to me, it was a baby "fix." My arms literally ached as we would drive home afterwards. I was so empty.

Every time the phone rang, another former high school friend was calling to say they were expecting. We graduated kindergarten together. In middle school, we giggled about boys we liked. In high school, we made our college plans and cried as we pried our arms from around one another after graduation. While in college, we met during Christmas breaks to reminisce and compare classes. We stood by each other's sides in bridesmaids dresses and waved goodbye as we drove off with our new grooms. Now, they were taking the next step in life: having babies. I was left on the "marriage square" of the Life game board. I would squeal with delight when they called with their good news, but when I would push "end" on the receiver, I would sit back and wait. Sometimes I would be able to walk in the other room and tell Jason, "They're going to have a baby! I wonder who it will look like?" Other times I collapsed on the bed and struggled to keep Jason from hearing my cries. As wonderful as he was, he simply could not understand the agony inside me. Without my helpmate, I faced this monster alone.

Then, there were the "unfit mothers," as I deemed them. I once saw a woman standing on the steps of a hospital, smoking. It would not have been so bad if her hospital gown wasn't swollen with a soon-to-be-born gift. I wanted to scream, "If you don't want that baby, I'll take it! How could you be so selfish?"

Around our small town I would run into people who would ask, "So when are y'all gonna have a baby?"

I would smile and say, "We already have one. She is a chocolate and tan weenie dog named Penelope." I mean, the nerve of these people! Was my life not satisfying enough for them? A few years earlier they had been asking, "When are you and Jason getting married?" Now, they were ready for me to spit out a baby months after walking down the aisle; and you know what? Then they would have talked about me for being pregnant before we got married. Ah, the life of small-town America! Obviously, that anger issue I used to have toward those who stared at my walking had crept back up and was now manifesting itself in the glares I gave undeserving women and too-inquisitive people.

"Why God? Why is this fair? Jason and I are good people. Why do they get a child, and we don't?" When I did not receive an answer from God, I just wrote it down in my mental notebook and said I would ask Him when I got to heaven. Right after I asked Him, "Why does de ja vu happen?" and "Why did you make men and women so radically different?"

Oh, now I had it all figured out. "I get what You are up to, God," I believed. This is what I deserved because we had chosen to ignore what God commands of his people who are not yet married. Not only was I certain of God's justice, but I was also certain of His wrath (so I imagined), which made me want to draw away from

Him. I became scared of Him and now did not feel comfort in His arms. I realized the disappointment I caused God. I imagined Him looking down at me and shaking His head in frustration. I was so ashamed.

Shame, however, is not of my Lord. (Romans 10:11, New International Version) "As the Scripture says, 'Anyone who trusts in Him will never be put to shame.'" God, in His infinite mercy, allowed me to read a Christian fiction book whose characters faced, and chose, the same mistake that Jason and I had. Their choice sent them into a whirlwind of consequences, which were never God's plan for their lives. Although they suffered immensely because of their wrong decision, when they confessed their sin in the end, God was faithful to them and brought joy to their lives. That book spoke volumes to my heart. I am not sure the endometriosis or childlessness are consequences of our mistake, but I can stand on the promise of scripture which has become my life verse: "'For I know the plans I have for you,' declared the Lord. 'Plans to prosper and not to harm you, plans to give you hope and a future'" (Jeremiah 29:11, New International Version). I had mastered steps one through three of the seven stages of grief: shock and denial, pain and guilt, anger and bargaining; yes, I was ready to bid them all farewell. This bondage had already been broken when Jesus tore lose my chains and saved me from hell! I was ready to have hope again, and I desperately needed to know that God was still the author of my future.

Chapter 23

I had one friend who did understand my pain. She and her husband had been trying for years to have a child but had no success. Often we had talked about the jealousy we had experienced when others shared news of their joy. I never thought about what would happen when that jealousy would turn on her.

Our church was beginning a study of spiritual gifts. We kicked off the weekend-long event with a meal. (We do look for any good reason to eat! After all, we live in the South—not the land flowing with milk and honey but instead, the land oozing with sweet tea and fried chicken.) While there in the fellowship hall, my friend and her husband walked in. (She and I had, unfortunately, not been as close because her husband, a preacher, had been called to an interim position a few miles up the road, and we didn't get to spend time together often.) She whispered something to our pastor, and his reaction let me know it was an exciting secret.

"They are going to have a baby!" my pastor screamed to the crowd.

Forks dropped and cheers erupted. The only thing that I dropped was my jaw. My throat fought a fierce battle with the cries that were rising up in it. Swallow. Gulp. I lost. I rushed to the bathroom just before a wail seeped from my mouth. My sister was right behind me. She held me tight against her shoulder so as to stifle the moans. Her strong arms wrapped around my convulsing shoulders.

"It's ok. It's ok. Shhh..." she whispered.

My mom and sister escorted me into the sanctuary when it was time for the first lesson of the weekend to begin. I had no idea what that guest speaker was talking about. All his opening jokes sounded ridiculous to me. I was miserable being there. Silent tears streamed down my face. I did not even care if anyone was watching. That poor man probably thought they needed to sing a quick verse or two of "Just As I Am" and let me have it out at the altar. Well, maybe I did need to go, but at that moment, the only place I wanted to go was home. I needed to make a break for it quickly. Who wanted to get stuck afterwards talking to everyone? I might risk coming face to face with my friend...the one who was pregnant. The one who had run off and left me behind in this stage of life. (I was a horrible friend, I know. She, however, was gracious enough to remember the pain we had both previously felt and forgave me for my selfishness.)

Once in the parking lot, Jason asked me if I wanted to go to the grocery store with him. "Yeah sure. Let's frolic through the aisles of frozen foods. Let's go gawk at all the choices of cereal. Ummm... let me think about this...no!" I thought. I did not have the heart to say it. He was obviously aware that I was broken down, but he still explained that he did not feel this way about our friends having a child.

"Just take me home, please," I said weakly.

I did need to be home alone. I wanted to be able to scream and cry in privacy, thank you very much. Flinging myself across the bed, I began to wail. (I'm sure you are wondering if I was near dehydration by this point. I thought so myself.) As I was lying there, my eyes landed on my Bible, which was on my nightstand. Placing it on my pillow, I had no idea what book to turn to. I decided to play "Bible roulette." The pages landed somewhere in Psalms. I laid my face in the Bible and cried out to the Lord.

"Please God. Show me something. I need to hear from You. I need a promise for *my* life," I begged.

Placing my head sideways, I breathed out a sigh to end my prayer. I was worn out. As if on cue, the page in the Bible turned with the exhale of my breath. Could it be for a reason? Was this the page I was supposed to read? I was desperate for any word from God.

I found the strength to lift my head. The curiosity was too much for me. My eyes landed on the verse.

"'Sing, barren woman, you who never bore a child; burst into song, shout for joy, you who were never in labor; because more are the children of the desolate woman than of her who has a husband,'" says the LORD.

"'Enlarge the place of your tent, stretch your tent curtains wide, do not hold back; lengthen your cords, strengthen your stakes. For you will spread out to the right and to the left; your descendants will dispossess nations and settle in their desolate cities'" (Isaiah 54:1-3, New International Version).

The Lord spoke straight to me. His word severed the tension around my heart. This was my promise. I would have my need to love a child fulfilled. I would have several children. His word said so. I wanted to cry out in thankfulness, but my eyes were dry. When God wipes away the tears, there are no leaks.

Shortly following that night, for the first time in my life, this barren woman began to sing in the choir; not long after, opportunities came for me to sing solos. I had much to sing about. It is easy when the Lord gives you a new song.

Chapter 24

Although I loved my teaching job, I really began to give myself whole-heartedly to it after the promise was made. Somehow, I got a feeling in my gut (which had gotten much bigger after I got married, by the way) that God was going to fulfill this promise, in some way, through school. I felt this with such confidence that I often mentioned it to friends. The promise in Isaiah 54: 1-3 goes on to command: "Do not be afraid; you will not be put to shame. Do not fear disgrace; you will not be humiliated" (Isaiah 54:4, New International Version). If I was going to believe it, I was going to believe it all.

At school I started giving more to my students. After all, I had been given a great example in my college professor, right? Against the advice of other educators, I dove into the lives of my students, making myself available if they needed to talk or be guided back onto the right path. Sometimes, that opened me up to heartbreak as they told me of drug-addicted mothers, fathers who were in jail, or parents who were struggling to feed their family. There have been times I have had to report incidences to the school counselor and other times to the Department of Human Services. Although difficult, I always knew that my goal was their future not their feelings at that moment. (High school students' feelings fluctuate every five minutes anyway, so you really cannot base decisions on that.)

I also began to share more of my own life with my students. This actually came because of the advice of a seventh grade student.

She was a tough nut to crack. She had lived a hard life and had recently moved to this area, which she was not very thrilled about.

"I am going to get her to like me," I thought. "She will WANT to work hard for me before I get finished with her."

I should have tried to train a bull before I attempted this feat. Her evil glares and snide remarks bucked me off time and time again. I got back up and got back on though.

One day, I decided to get brave enough to touch the bull, I mean the girl, on the shoulder.

"Don't touch me!" she screamed as she stormed out of the room.

I followed her down the hall, at a good distance behind. (I'm not crazy. I thought she might hit me.) I found her, fuming mad, on the floor of the tile bathroom.

My first thought was, "Gag a maggot! Get off that nasty bathroom floor!" But I knew I did not want her to get up and move anywhere else. It wasn't like I could run after her!

I sat down beside her. High heels and black pants next to her worn out tennis shoes and bulky hooded sweatshirt.

"What's wrong?" I asked.

"I just have a lot going on, and you are always on me," she explained.

"I have some things going on myself." (This was during the first time we found out Daddy had cancer.) "I just found out my daddy has cancer."

She looked me in the eye and with all the wisdom of a grown woman she said, "Maybe if you didn't act like such a hard*** and let us know what is going on with you, we would be kinder to you."

I cried. I did not punish her or send her to the office, although I was thinking, "Ah, she just cussed!" I remained calm with the bull. Her advice had made an impact on me. It made perfect sense. Kids need to know that they are not alone in the world with their problems. Duh, you would think I would be an expert on this lesson by now.

So with that bathroom conversation and my promise from God, I began to allow myself to be vulnerable with my students. Their writing changed. Suddenly, they wanted to hang around after class to talk. Sometimes, during break, I thought I needed to hand out numbers in the "advice line." "Now serving ticket number five, ticket number five!"

A creative writing student began to talk to me about the fight she and her mom had that morning. Kids were often obviously affected during the day if their morning at home was out of routine. This girl was hurt and felt that her little sister, who suffered from a disease, got all the attention in the family. In her mind, she believed, they could not see how she was falling apart and needed them to hold her together. I sat at my desk. She sat in the floor at my feet. I had no words, so I just grabbed her head and laid it in my lap. I leaned my body over her head and patted her back. Her sobbing slowly snuffed out. It was at that moment that I realized how much helping her and petting her helped fill the emptiness in my own heart and arms.

I have found that students often just need to be seen as people and not as haircuts, colors, or clothes. So many times, adults stereotype kids more than their peers do. "He's a sissy," they might say because a boy does not not play sports, or "She's a goth," they will sneer at the color of a girl's clothes. It is an injustice. Kids should never have to stand up to adults. We should be the examples. Often Valerie and I (who, by the way, teaches English at the same school) vie for those students when it comes to recommendations for awards or scholarships. I still remember what it was like to be "different," and I also recall how it felt being recognized as worthy when I received the honor of class president my senior year.

My sister Valerie and me in my classroom.

In addition to giving advice, teaching allows us so many opportunities to help kids. I am amazed at the teachers around me who so quickly give money to help girls find that perfect prom dress, boys to choose dress shoes to wear with their caps and gowns, students to obtain a yearbook, or a family to buy necessities after a house fire. I am inspired. How could a job that does not offer much in salary be filled by so many individuals who are willing to give? I was thankful that I worked with not only great people but also obedient Christians.

I began telling kids "I love you" more often. I never want the meaning of the words to be lost. I mean it. God has given me such a love for these kids and this job that I cannot help letting the words come from the overflow of my heart.

God also gave my family two other blessings to love during this time. Valerie's ashes got even more beautiful as she and her husband Jeff gave birth first to a baby girl. They gave her the name Elliana, which means "God has answered me." Oh, how He had answered our family with this child. She is tender-hearted and cries when she sees others hurting. Elli is a submissive rule-follower and will one day, I am convinced, be an obedient worker for Christ. Cooper came along eighteen months later. His hazel eyes squint when he grins just as my father's did. I like to believe Daddy helped hand pick Cooper's eyes and Elli's naturally curly hair. "Coop" is a jokester who loves being at the center of attention. Maybe he will use his personality to draw others to the Lord.

Aunt Nene telling "spooky" stories (that end being funny) with Cooper and Elliana.

During this time, Jason and I talked about the possibility of adopting. Our sweet niece and nephew needed cousins to play with, right? I think I liked the idea better than he did. He would say, "I just don't know how you could love a child that isn't your own. Well, maybe you would love them, but would it be as much as if it were yours?"

I thought so, but of course, I had never been there, done that, so how was I to know? As we discussed this further, I felt that I was pushing the issue with him. God gave me the discernment to know to come to Him about this instead of talking Jason's ear off. I began to pray that whatever our decision was to be in the future, Jason and I would be on the same page.

"God, if this is not what You have planned, please take this idea of adoption away from me. Make me feel the same way that Jason does. I know that You will not call us to do anything that we disagree about. You will give the dream to both of us."

One day while Jason and I were riding around, I mentioned that I believed that God would grant us a child through my teaching. Now in my mind I imagined an elementary school child or maybe even one of my high school students who had gotten pregnant and wanted to give the baby up for adoption. (It always seemed like I had them in my classroom anyway. "Great, God. Are you just trying to test my patience?" I would think. "Oh, oh never mind God. I did not say anything about testing patience! Please erase that from Your infinite memory as far as east is from west.")

How Jason responded shocked me: "What if right now, somewhere, God is preparing a child just for us?"

As I stared across the dashboard of his Dodge Ram, a scene of hope began to paint itself on the horizon. I imagined a woman making, what she thought, was a mistake and a child coming forth as a result. Little did I know that mistakes were being made by a woman, but it would not be a child who would bear the marks of those errors…it would be a young man.

Chapter 25

There was a senior in Valerie's English class called Bubba. (Yes, "Bubba" feeds every Southern stereotype, but the nickname was given to him by his sisters when they were younger and could not say "brother.") Because of the behind-the-scenes working of God, my sister felt drawn to him. He was not a stellar student, nor did he warmly welcome others into his life except for his few closest friends. If he was not angry about something, he was sleeping. Walking down the hall, he dared anyone to look his way or to brush against him. When Valerie told me that God had placed him on her heart I thought, "Great, another bull."

I decided to help her pray for him. If she was that drawn to him, then the least I could do was ask God to use Valerie to reach Bubba. To be honest, I prayed, but it was not with fervency, only whenever it crossed my mind. Valerie, on the other hand, was writing his name every morning in her devotional. Its pages were filled with concerns for Bubba's salvation, Bubba's attitude, and Bubba's home life.

Valerie began to go one step further by sparking discussions with him at school. Soon, she was asking me to pray more specifically as their discussions had revealed his intense anger towards a God who allowed him to experience such a hard life. What was that life? We didn't know yet. That was too personal, and she learned to peel back Bubba's layers a little at a time.

A thick layer was peeled off one day during a Fellowship of Christian Students meeting at school. Now, typically, we average 200-300 high school students per gathering. We understand that many of them only come because it gets them out of the classroom during our scheduled club time, but we know that God will use the time, so we do not worry about WHY they are attending. On this day, I led the devotion. Its premise was to show the students that we are all more alike than different. As the bell rang and the students cleared the gym to go home, one student remained: Bubba. Valerie went to talk to him. I left because I knew that too many wranglers in the ring can sometimes spook the bull.

As she spoke with him about God's love for him, she explained, "Bubba, if you were bleeding, I would take you to the hospital. You have a hole in your heart, and the only One who can fix it is the Great Physician."

He only answered her in tears. There were no words of negativity, no fits of disbelief. Hey, that was a start, right?

One evening while on our cell phones, Valerie and I discussed him.

"I feel like we are supposed to do more for this kid," she expressed.

"Could we help him with his senior year expenses? Or maybe I should just take him home with me," I joked.

"Maybe so," she laughed. "Let's just pray about what we are supposed to do."

That night, at Jason's mom's house, I flopped across her bed while she and Jason worked on the computer.

"So what if I bring a kid home with me?" I nonchalantly threw out there.

Immediately, both their heads turned from the computer screen. "What?" they both said.

I did my best to explain his personality, but I did not have that many details. "I don't know. Maybe we could help him in some way though."

At home the next afternoon, I laid out another option for Jason, "It's his senior year and winter will be coming up soon. What if we get him a letterman's jacket? He plays football, and all his other friends have one."

In fact, I think I was still feeling embarrassed for sticking my foot in my mouth his junior year when I had him in my English class. The day his friends had received their jackets, they were all standing around, excitedly comparing patches and chevrons. I had asked, "When are you getting yours, Bubba?"

"I'm not," he growled as if I had taken the spot light off them and placed it across his bare back.

Jason agreed, and I did not hesitate. Right then, we got in the car and drove to our local sporting goods store. They actually had pictures of his friends' jackets on the wall, so I was able to get patches that exactly matched theirs. Letterman's jackets take months to get back, so we paid our down payment and agreed to continue to come back and make payments. (Hey, those things are expensive!)

As God would have it, Bubba was also enrolled in my creative writing class at the same time he was in Valerie's English class. He was a good writer whose vivid imagination produced great fiction stories. It was not his fiction that impressed me; it was his personal writing. Often, he laid his emotions on the blue lines of his composition notebook. I was eager to know what events his words alluded to, yet I was too scared to ask.

One morning, on the way to school, I decided to get serious about praying for Bubba.

"I'm sorry, God. I know that I have been flippant about my prayers. I want to get serious with you and obey what You tell me to do. Whatever You say, God, I'm ready." The answer I received, in return, gave me the feeling that this obedience was going to be big and it could involve the basement of my house.

As I ended my prayer, a song came on the radio that I had never heard. The voices of Nichole Nordeman and Selah blended together. Nichole's opening words pierced me. They seemed to fit Bubba's needs:

"One day, eyes that are blind will see You clearly,
and one day all who deny will finally believe.
One day hearts made of stone will break in pieces,
and one day chains once unbroken will fall down at your feet,
so we wait for that one day, come quickly.
We want to see Your glory..."

I began to cry as I listened to the words. I praised God for assuring me that Bubba's hard heart could be broken. I knew that his tongue, as well as every other tongue, would one day declare Jesus as Lord (Romans 14:11). I did want that day to come quickly. I just did not know it would be so soon.

This morning just happened to be on a Thursday. On those mornings at our school, some of the teachers come together for a short devotion. No one else needed to show up that day. The words God had given the devotion leader were spoken only to me. He spoke of the faith Noah had in building the ark. It had never rained before; yet this man was not fazed by the questions or laughter of others. He simply followed God. Noah trusted God to equip him to do that which He had called him to do.

I was having a come-to-Jesus meeting in the back of that classroom. The message was so clear to me. God might as well have told me to build an ark. But He didn't. Instead He said, "Do not worry what others will say. Do not worry about your job. Nia, I have blessed you and Jason with a house that has a basement where this boy could live. Offer it to him."

I walked around that morning in a trance. All I could see was God's message. Never mind the MINOR detail that I had not even discussed this with Jason. (Seriously discussed it and heard his answer.) Never mind that Bubba had not even talked to me personally as he had Valerie. I just, somehow, confidently knew that God would open the door for Bubba to walk right inside.

Chapter 26

That same day, as God scrolled His plan on a blimp in front of my eyes, Bubba asked if he could stay back and talk to me instead of going to the lunchroom.

"Sure," I said. ("Ahh! God! He wants to talk! He has never talked to me before...")

He propped himself against my lateral file cabinet, crossed his arms tightly, and began to cry.

"I feel like I don't have anywhere to go. I live with my best friend right now, but his dad already has two boys and a daughter and is taking care of them alone after his wife died. He can't afford for me to live with them. I feel like I'm wearing out my welcome."

I tried to act calm, "Why aren't you living at home anyway? Or why couldn't you go to a relative's house?"

He told me that he and his mother fought a couple of months prior, and she had attacked him violently. (Out of respect for Bubba's privacy and his family's, I need to spare details.)

"It was the last straw. I have taken enough throughout my life, and I'm old enough that I don't have to keep living like that. I can't go live with other family members because lots of them do drugs or did do them in the past. My dad was an alcoholic when I was growing up, and when I used to live with him, we never had enough to eat," he explained. "I just don't know what to do, Mrs. Stivers. I just don't have anywhere to go."

Was he really saying this? Was this really happening? Again, why was I shocked that God had prepared me for this? I wonder how many more miracles I could be a part of if only I were willing to look for His hands at work and try to become a pair of gloves.

"Bubba, I know that what I'm about to say is going to sound crazy, but bear with me. I have been praying about how I could help you. God has told me to offer you our home. We have a basement, so you could feel like you were separate from us. Jason and I can't have children of our own, and maybe this is the reason. Of course, I have not talked to my husband about this yet, but I have to say it because this is what God told me to say." The words seemed to spew from me like a shaken soda bottle while Bubba stared at me like I was an idiot.

"That's really nice, but you are my teacher and that would just be weird. I appreciate you offering. It means a lot, but no thanks," he answered.

"Well, at least let me help you with money," I retorted. "I heard that you have been stealing food from the gas station after football practice. Bubba, the last thing you need is to be arrested. I'm going to go there and pay a tab for you. When you go to the counter, tell them your name, and get what you want. I'll check on the money once a week and add more when it's needed. Now don't buy for the whole football team. We don't have that much money!"

"That's nice. But I don't need any help from anybody," he replied.

As Bubba left the room to go to lunch, I looked up. "Ok God. What was up with this? I did what You told me to do. I feel so stupid.

Maybe I said all that too soon." I heard no reply from God but only sensed the steadfast conviction I had felt that morning.

That evening I dropped the news on a poor, unsuspecting husband. I told him the story and asked him to pray about it. He went outside to mow. God must reveal answers in the smell of freshly cut grass because when Jason came back in he stated, "If this is what God is telling you to do. I'll support you." Whew, he was a good hubby.

Weeks afterward were spent trying to gain Bubba's trust. Like a beautiful gift being unwrapped, he began to share more and more of himself. He had even given in and allowed me to start a tab at the gas station. Jason and I went to every football game that season. (We had NEVER done that before.) I even bought a shirt with Bubba's jersey number on the back.

As winter's icy winds began to chill us, Jason and I knew it was time to give Bubba his letterman's jacket. It was finally ready at the sporting goods store, and I was eager to see that school mascot across his back. I had no wrapping paper except for last year's Christmas paper. It would work. Snowmen are cute all the time!

"Santa came early," I told him one night before taking him out to meet his friends for dinner.

He was so unsuspecting, and I was so emotional. (Imagine that!) It seemed to take him forever to release the tape off each corner of the wrapping.

"Come on with it!" I wanted to scream, but I knew that opening presents was not something he often got to savor.

As he flipped the lid off the bulging shirt box, he sat with his head in his hands. He could not even pick up the jacket. He hated that he was crying in front of me AND Jason, but the meaning of the gift was too much for him. As he stood up and slung it around his shoulders, he grabbed the bottom seams of the jacket to straighten himself up. His chest puffed out and his grin said, "Look at me!" Then, he came to us and thanked us with words that seemed too few in his mind. He could have said nothing. The way he strutted around in that jacket was "thank you" enough to the two of us.

One proud teenager strutting around in his new letterman's jacket.

One week he asked me to help him make a poster board of pictures of him. The posters were to be displayed on senior night at the after-game reception. I gathered poster board and my classroom's bulletin board border and letters. I wanted his to be the best one. He should be proud of something, for once. I also saw this as an opportunity to let him get to know Jason and me a little better.

"Why don't you come home with me one evening? That way we can work on making your poster."

He agreed, and I was as nervous as a long-tailed cat in a room full of rocking chairs. Jason was to bring pizza home for supper. As we stood in the kitchen, waiting for Jason to get home from work, Bubba did something that let me know he was beginning to trust me. He showed me his prized notebook that contained his most private feelings. I did not read every one, though I wanted to. I read a few entries that he pointed out, but I knew this moment was not about what was contained in those pages but instead, the trust that was now being shared between the two of us.

We worked on his poster board, filling it with pictures and royal blue lettering spelling "Bubba" down the side. He was thrilled and looked forward to showing it off on Friday night. We ate pizza together in the living room. Jason and he shared little conversation that was not about football. Of course, I was lost. It did not matter. My mind was too busy imagining this as my family.

Senior night was hard. Bubba had struggled with asking his mom and step dad to walk him out onto the field. As much as I wished it were Jason and me, they were his family. I watched from the bleachers and clapped and smiled. From the outside, I looked like I had it all together.

Bubba's family did not stay for the reception. He was broken-hearted. Family was what senior night was about. Although he and his younger brother would both be emerging from the locker room after the game, they only waited for his brother, then turned and made their way to their car. Jason and I went to the reception instead. Although he bounced around, taking pictures with his friends, I saw him look over his shoulder a few times to make sure we were still there. It would take a few more acts on our part to show him what reliability looked like.

Chapter 27

We helped Bubba study for his driver's permit. Typically, fifteen year olds get them. He was nineteen. We even had to take him to Tennessee to get a copy of his birth certificate from a government office. Little by little, we were showing Bubba we cared about helping him to become a productive member of society, but he had already planned that future for himself.

The summer before his senior year, Bubba had signed up for the Army Infantry. He wanted the most dangerous job because, at that point, he did not care about his life. As sad as that was, we were thankful that he had made future plans to better himself. That was noble.

We invited him to Jason's mother's house for dinner one night. He came to a family gathering at my grandfather's. He was amazed that at those houses, no one was passed out drunk in the floor or fighting. When Bubba said that, I looked at him like he had three heads. I realized that my family had been blessed by God, but I had never thought that we were blessed in that we got along with one another!

Before Bubba could become a part of our family, he needed to know some ground rules first. Another night when he agreed to spend the night with us, Jason went to pick him up. He told Bubba that if he did decide to come and live in our house, there were going to be rules that he would follow. He would have a curfew as well as be expected to make good grades. We were active members of our church, and he would be there with us. Taking him in would also require trust on our part, and Jason told him that if he put us in danger or disrespected us, he would not be allowed to live there anymore. Jason trusted him with me, and if he had any ill-mannered ideas, he would be asked to leave.

Bubba said he understood, but he still had not accepted our invitation. It would take a different kind of invitation.

Our church's youth group was taking a trip to a judgment house, which is a walk-through dramatization that depicts how the choice to accept Jesus as your Lord and Savior can either lead to heaven or to hell. We invited Bubba and one of his friends to go with us. I knew this could be a crucial night. He was still angry with God for the life he had "been given," yet, he had heard me say over and over that the same God had called me to ask him to come and live with us.

During the judgment house, I could tell he was attentive. He took in every word, every scripture, and every depiction. Heaven was beautiful to him, but hell was frightening. At the end of the walk-through, Bubba and I were separated within the crowd that was being led into a room where a youth pastor gave a little of his own testimony. Then, he offered an invitation for anyone to pray to receive Christ as their personal King. When the prayer was over, everyone was ushered into the sanctuary. I was a little disappointed that Bubba had not made a decision to pray that prayer. As we walked out, I kept asking, "Where's Bubba? Has anyone seen Bubba?"

"He's back there in another room praying with someone," another youth member told me.

I immediately started to sweat. Oh, how I wanted to run as I darted back through the corridors of the hallway, trying to find him. Suddenly, I turned a corner and stumbled into him. He wrapped his arms around me and fell onto my shoulder, crying out the sins of his past. Nothing else mattered in that moment. The prodigal son, my chosen son and now God's son, had come home.

Chapter 28

Bubba carried his Bible to school with him the next day. Instead of sleeping in class, he spent time reading the Word and writing down scripture that spoke to him. His voice bubbled as he told other students what had happened to him the previous night. Here was the boy who did not want anyone to speak to him now speaking the Truth to anyone who would listen. I was beaming with pride.

"I think I'll come and live with you after football season," he told me one day.

"Ugh, ok!" I cried.

Bubba told me that he had prayed specifically for some new blue jeans when he got home from the judgment house. His others were filled with holes and were getting too small. The following evening, a friend brought over an entire bag of blue jeans and dumped them out in front of Bubba's unbelieving eyes. "Do you want any of these jeans? They are all too small for me, or I just never wore them," his friend said.

Bubba was thrilled not only about the jeans but also about his first answered prayer. The words from the song played again in my head: "One day eyes that are blind will see you clearly." He was seeing the Lord at work in his life.

That Sunday, he agreed to go to church with us. At the end of the service, our pastor called Bubba and me to the front. Our pastor laid his mighty arm around Bubba and proceeded to tell the congregation that Bubba had been saved on the previous Sunday. As the thunderous claps settled, I asked the church's support as Bubba was about to come and live with us. That church family never hesitated in loving us. Why would they hesitate to love him?

I spent days getting the basement ready to become his room. I guess I was "nesting," as new mothers do, before a baby comes home. It was my only chance to get a "nursery" ready.

Our school counselor bought Bubba some hygiene products such as razors, deodorant, and shampoo, and I bought some plastic stackable drawers where he could store his clothes. Valerie and my mom bought all his favorite snacks. The finishing touch was a poster board sign that proclaimed, "Welcome home, Bubba."

He came to live with us on Halloween of 2007. He and his friends handed out our candy and scared away passers-by with their gory costumes. Ahh, teenage boys. Our house was definitely going to be a different place.

Thanksgiving came and went. I could not wait until Christmas. I wanted to share all of our family traditions with him. It was exciting to wrap presents for him to find under the tree when I knew what his past Christmases had been like. The local fire department had always held Christmas drives for his community, so when he was younger, Bubba began to equate Christmas with the fire hall. Yes, the holidays would be different for him now, but could we keep his attention without a shiny red fire truck?

Christmas Eve was scary. His family called him unexpectedly and wanted to see him. We could not keep him from his family at

Christmas, so we took him to meet his sister. She would then take him to his family's house. He made it back an hour late for our family functions that night. As we drove to my mother's house, he said words that stole my excitement away much like the Grinch stole Whoville's presents.

"I'm thinking that I might go back home to live. They were really nice tonight, and my mother apologized for what happened. I really miss my brothers and sisters. I can't thank you enough for all you've done, but that's my family," he explained as tenderly as possible.

"No, no. I understand. We can't keep you from that decision if that's what you want to do. Just please promise me one thing, Bubba. Pray about it before you make any decisions," I answered calmly. I was not calm on the inside.

That night as I lay in the bed, I told Jason what Bubba had told me.

"Nia, we did what God told us to do, but we can't make Bubba accept it. We offered him this place so he would have a warm home and something to fill his belly. We can't keep him here," Jason reasoned.

I did not want reasoning! I wanted Bubba to stay! I was terrified that his family was telling him only what he wanted to hear. What if he went back into that home and was hurt even more, physically or mentally? It was another night of stifled sobs as I tried to keep from waking Jason. I begged God to give Bubba the right answer. If he was supposed to go home, God was going to have to speak peace to my heart quickly. I was sure it was exploding.

"Surely God, You did not ask us to step out on faith, only for it to end months later. I just do not believe this is our entire story."

I cried myself to sleep, only to wake up to an anxious teenage boy knocking on our door.

"Wake up! Wake up! It's time to open presents!" he screamed.

As we took our places on the couch and began to give out gifts, he looked at me.

"Nia, I prayed last night about going back home."

I stopped breathing.

"I want to stay. God told me this is where I need to be."

Last night, while I was upstairs begging for God's mercy, downstairs, He was whispering an answer to my prayer in Bubba's ear. I was so thankful I received such a gift.

However, the best gift I received came after Bubba had settled in with us for a few months. He had some "girl trouble," and he and I had gone to get some ice cream and talk it over. (Bubba believed in ice cream solving problems like I believe in hot baths.)

When we pulled back into the driveway, he looked seriously at me. "Nia, I need to tell you something. Do you remember the Thursday I came to talk to you at school and tell you that I felt like I had nowhere to go?"

"Do I remember that Thursday? Umm, yeah…I think I do." (He could understand my sarcasm. God knew I did not need a small child.)

"Well that night I was planning on committing suicide. I had already decided how I was going to do it and everything. I only came to you that day because I wanted someone to know, after I killed myself, what I was going through. I knew that you would be able to tell other people what I had said. But when you told me that God had told you to offer your basement, I thought, 'Somebody cares.' True, I thought you were crazy, and I had no intention of coming to live with you, but it gave me hope. I decided not to kill myself after I talked to you."

Now I had experienced confirmation from the Lord before, but never before had I felt God reach down and pat me on the shoulder. His voice whispered in my ear, "See, now do you understand? This is what I had planned." I could not say a word to Bubba. I just stared at the steering wheel and cried. Bubba cried too. We both mourned about what could have happened and rejoiced in what had not.

I learned such a lesson that night. Bubba's life had been at risk. Although it was not me who saved him, I got to have a part in God's plan. I felt humbled and undeserving. God is good, all the time. Even when we do not know what He has up His robe's sleeves.

Chapter 29

W e would never regret having Bubba (our "chosen" son, as we began to call him to those who did not know the story); however, going from not having a child to raising a teenager was hard. He was still quick tempered. He seemed to dwell on the negatives in life. His outlook and reasoning were just different than ours. We had to keep in mind that he had seen and experienced such an opposite childhood than we had. I began to realize that nature wins over nurture in some cases. I could not, in a few months' time, erase nineteen years worth of hurt.

At times, parenting Bubba was like breaking a wild horse. Only once did he come home late. (It was ten minutes late, and we were both waiting up. He was not allowed to go out again the next time. I guess my Mama turned out to be smart because I was becoming just like her, and goodness, I was pretty brilliant!) When he failed a class, he was grounded. If he continued to text girls that we believed were not good influences for him, he got his cell phone taken away. Whew, did he buck on that one! You would have thought we took oxygen away. Heck, just months ago he did not even have a cell phone until we got him one for Christmas. My, how fast they forget. (I'm so glad we are not like that with God. Cough, cough...)

We quickly learned that there would be many skills, among life lessons, that we would teach Bubba. Here, Jason teaches him to tie a necktie on our first Easter Sunday morning together.

When he finally broke up with his girlfriend of two years, we were worried about him. Jason was scared because there was a gun cabinet in the basement. Although we did not believe he was suicidal now, Jason and I decided we did not want to take any chances with our precious occupant. We went downstairs to remove the boxes of bullets and make sure the cabinet was locked. We found him sitting on his bed, shuffling through photos and letters he had shared with his girlfriend.

Jason's voice broke the silence, "I know that you think we are hard on you, Bubba. Yes, we pushed for this breakup. You have to understand that we made a promise to God to take care of you and lead you to Him in everything. I know you are hurting right now because you loved her, but we will always be here for you. We will be your family, if you will let us."

Bubba stood up, grabbed Jason, and cried on his shoulder. Although no words were said in that moment, it seemed to seal the deal not only for Jason but also for Bubba.

Up until this point, Jason had not allowed himself to fall in love with Bubba as I had much earlier. Jason believed we were simply providing for him while he was in school, and when he graduated, he would go into the Army and become self sufficient. Sure, they watched football and played video games together, but what guys did not?

Bubba wanted to go outside and burn some of the pictures and letters. He was ready to close that chapter of his life.

"Want me to go out and help you?" Jason offered.

"Yeah, if you don't care," Bubba replied.

I knew that this was their bonding moment. I just went back upstairs and prayed for their budding relationship. We had come full circle; my relationship with Jason had begun because of a break up, and Jason's relationship with Bubba began because of one. I think Jason now had his answer to the question, "Can you possibly love a child who is not your own?"

Our first "family" photo with Bubba.

Chapter 30

$\mathcal{G}$raduation night came, and I was on the field as a teacher/ senior sponsor, while Jason was in the crowded stands, attempting to take pictures. We met some of Bubba's family that night. His father, grandmother, aunt, and sister were there to support him. His mother was not.

Bubba proudly took me to meet them after the ceremony. (I took Valerie with me. I was afraid of how they would react to me.) His family had already made their way to their car, on the other side of the chain-linked fence bordering the football field. As I stuck my hand through a diamond-pattered hole to shake his grandmother's hand, she continued to hold on to me.

"I can't begin to tell you how much we appreciate what you have done for Bubba. I really don't know where he'd be if it were not for you. I wonder if he would have graduated tonight at all."

I was humbled at her words. Where would *he* be? Goodness, where would *I* be had God not intervened in my life when I was fifteen?

Jason and I were not sad about graduation night. It was June 16 that was looming. That was the day he would leave for basic training.

It came too soon. Bubba had spent many of the last few weeks of "freedom" with his friends. We understood, but we were somewhat sad because that meant our time with him was even less. We also noticed that he seemed to be pulling away from God during this time. I hated the thoughts of his leaving the safety of home and our home church. Would this military lifestyle help foster a love for the Lord?

I wrote him a letter the morning we were to take him to the Army recruiting station. I wanted to try to put into words how we loved him and to offer a few inspirational scriptures too. While we waited for the bus to come and take him away from us, I tried to keep myself together.

Jason had warned me, "Now it isn't going to make it any easier on him if you break down. You can cry when we get in the car." Hmph, such a man.

The bus got there too soon, in my mind. It was time for me to let him go. We had only had him seven and a half short months. That was not even long enough to carry a baby to term. Now, I had to let him go for the greater cause of our country. It was noble, I know, but it did not make it any easier.

I handed him my letter. He handed me one in return. Jason hugged him and told him how proud he was of him. Now, it was my turn.

"Well, give me a hug," Bubba said playfully.

When he stepped onto that bus, our lives together would never be the same. He would be stationed here and there and even face deployment. He would no longer be under our watch care. Our entrustment from the Lord was over. I allowed my hug to linger while I considered all these thoughts. When I let go, I handed him back to God, got in the car, turned my face to the window, and began to cry.

Chapter 31

*B*ubba wrote to us often during basic training. I was miserable not hearing his voice. Waiting eagerly by the mailbox several days each week, I tried to imagine his voice narrating the letters as it happens in movies. It did not work.

So many times, his letters described training or used jargon we could not understand. However, there was one part of his letters we always comprehended. Bubba was seeking out God for himself. He had found a group of soldiers who had worship services. He told us of songs he loved to sing and how he would close his eyes and feel the words. It reminded me of my time of falling in love with the Lord while at the Christian Student Organization in college. At one point, he even asked for a hymnal from our church, so they could have a wider variety of songs to sing. I was so thankful to know Bubba was still sensitive to God's spirit.

Bubba graduated from Fort Benning, Georgia, in August. We, along with his best friend and his father, were there to cheer him on. Jason got the distinct honor of pinning on his blue Infantry cords during the "Turning Blue" ceremony. This denoted that Bubba was officially trained as an Infantryman of the United States Army. To say we were proud would be an understatement.

Pinning on Bubba's Infantry cords was a proud moment for Jason.

December would not be as happy for us as the previous one had been. Bubba would leave for his first deployment to Afghanistan. We went to Fort Campbell, Kentucky, where he was now stationed, to spend time with him before he left. I was a wreck. I could not imagine him not being within driving distance if he needed us. Yes, basic training was hard, but at least he was safe in the United States. Although I did not want my mind to go to such places, the possibility of death was too much to avoid. I remembered telling my father goodbye, knowing I would never see him again. That had been the hardest thing I had ever done, but at least I prepared myself that his death was imminent. I did not want to prepare myself for Bubba's death. If I did that, the Army would have to pry my fingers from him as I would not be letting him go.

We ate lunch together on our last day with him. Jason was going to stay with him a little longer and drive Bubba's vehicle back to Alabama. I had to leave earlier to come home and sing in a

Christmas cantata at church. This barren woman would not feel like singing a song that night.

They walked me to my car. We tried to talk and put off that last hug, but our time was cut short by the blistering cold wind.

"Well, give me a hug." (It had become his signature saying in these times.)

As I hugged him I whispered, "Please God." Bubba never even heard my plea. The wind had picked it up and carried it off. It did not matter. The prayer was never meant for Bubba's ears. It was meant for the Creator of the wind.

I was thankful Jason and Bubba turned quickly to drive off for their extra time together. I myself could not turn the key in the ignition. I could not fasten my seatbelt. What I could do was beat the steering wheel…and scream.

Bubba's year in Afghanistan was long and hard on us but even harder on him. Although we did not get to talk often on the phone, we chatted/emailed over the blessing of the Internet almost every day. I could tell that being there was changing him. He was becoming hard-hearted again. I do not know what he saw in Afghanistan. I do not know what he experienced. I, at first, believed that if he wanted to tell me, I would listen. But if whatever that monster was had been bad enough to take away his ability to sleep, I did not want to meet it.

The Junior Holy Spirit side of me kicked in again. I could simply tell him how God wanted him to react, right? I pushed. I prodded. Bubba was patient, although it was obvious that he did not want to hear about God. At one point, I pushed him too far, I am ashamed to say.

He was dealing with a family situation. By this time in our relationship, these "situations" were a dime a dozen. Jason and I would become so frustrated with him for not being wise to their dramatic ways. He would fall right into the drama pit each time and wallow around with them.

"Do not go down this road again, Bubba," we would tell him. "When you start talking to one of them, then it is not long before someone has told a lie on you about what you did or did not say, then the process starts all over again."

I am thankful that I will never know what he has felt, but at the same time, it makes it so hard to understand his actions. Why kids, as well as adults, continue to go back to the ones who hurt them, I will never know. So many times, in the cases of kids at school who are abused, they will defend the abuser until the end, always choosing their side. Again, I have been blessed never to have had to face this dilemma.

So this time, when Bubba was worried about a situation with his family, I pushed the "truth policy" we share together (always to tell each other the utmost truth). The truth I offered in an email was probably just my control freak opinion.

He had never talked to me the way he did in that response. He even cussed. Now, that was a line crossed with me. I answered the email enough to tell him that I would be taking a break from contacting him. I would not stand for him to talk to me that way, no matter what the cause. I would be taking some time to sit back and pray about this.

I did not regret standing up and demanding respect in his language, but it did not take much praying before God started changing me. "Now that was not the plan, God! I was trying to help out the case for You, remember? It is Bubba You should be changing." I have since noticed that every time I pray for someone else to change, the Lord changes me instead.

"My dear child, don't shrug off God's discipline, but don't be crushed by it either. It's the child He loves that he disciplines; the child He embraces, He also corrects. God is educating you; that's why you must never drop out. He's treating you as dear children. This trouble you're in isn't punishment; it's training, the normal experience of children. Only irresponsible parents leave children to fend for themselves. Would you prefer an irresponsible God? We respect our own parents for training and not spoiling us, so why not embrace God's training so we can truly live? While we were children, our parents did what seemed best to them. But God is doing what is best for us, training us to live God's holy best. At the time, discipline isn't much fun. It always feels like it's going against the grain. Later, of course, it pays off handsomely, for it's the well-trained who find themselves mature in their relationship with God" (Hebrews 12:5-11, The Message).

I realized, through prayer and advice from one of my sorority sisters, that God did not need my help. Now it hurt to realize that. I was getting a heavenly whoopin'. The times in my life where I have changed my ol' sinful self have been when God Himself showed me the sin, not someone else. (Remember the drum major? I was doing the same thing!) As my pastor says, "When you see Your Savior, you see yourself. When you see yourself, you see your sin. When you see your sin, you cry out for grace and mercy." Bubba was not going to change because I told him what he was doing wrong. Bubba would change when God told him to change. Lesson learned.

In July, Bubba came home for a two-week R&R. Jason and I waited anxiously in the Atlanta airport for him. Veterans had an area marked off specifically for military families to wait. Tiny American flags waved. Children clung to camouflage teddy bears. Wives waited in beautiful dresses, their hair and makeup perfected. We all stood behind the red, white, and blue ropes, staring straight ahead at the escalators, which were rising to meet us. With every soldier's head that popped up as the movable staircase climbed, cheers erupted and families went running to greet them. It was quite a sight to see. I was proud of my country and how they welcomed home their troops.

Suddenly, I saw some familiar looking brown hair. This was another time that I wished I could run. I limped quickly to meet him, and he dropped his bag to receive my hug. As my face lay on the upper corner of his chest in a blur of camouflage and tears, I heard God say, "Here he is. I brought him home to you."

It was not only us who were waiting in the United States for Bubba. He now had a girlfriend, a classmate from high school, and one of the first students I ever taught. I actually had known "BJ" (yes, another nickname short for her first and last initials) longer than I had known Bubba. During his two weeks at home, she would become his fiancée.

His leaving to go back to Afghanistan was not as difficult as the first time. He would only be there four months before completing his deployment. Plus, I had come to realize that the Lord loved Bubba even more than I did. That was reason enough that he would be protected.

After Bubba returned overseas, I began getting to know BJ more as a person instead of just a former student. This four-foot-eleven blonde held power enough to handle Bubba yet was the most easy-going female I had ever known. Nothing seemed to ruffle her feathers. (Whew, I would be able to learn so much from her!) She was level headed and wise, and the Lord knew Bubba needed that.

I also soon realized, through asking her, that she believed in God but had never given Him her life. I began to talk to her about what God had done for me and offered to answer any questions she might have. For months she went to church with us when she was not scheduled to work. I was fighting back the Jr. Holy Spirit role and trusting that God was working on her in His own good time.

It was now October, and guess what opportunity would present itself? That's right. The same judgment house Bubba had gone to two years earlier. Again, we went with the youth group. Again, it was the same premise. She sat next to me in the final room as the youth pastor's testimony was given and the opportunity to pray to receive Christ was offered. This time, I had no doubts about the decision being made in that room. I felt her hand swish past my leg as she raised it to denote she wanted more information. I waited for her in the same spot where I had found Bubba. When she came out of the room, we embraced. It was almost a reenactment. I was in the presence of royalty--a princess to the King of Kings. And she would soon be my daughter.

Chapter 32

ubba was home from Afghanistan a little over a week before he and BJ got married. They chose to be married the day before our six-year wedding anniversary. They, too, stood on that same stage where God seemed to always bring our life circle back around. That night as the white lights glistened on the Christmas trees with the garland spread 'round the stage, the family members and friends who had long supported our God-adventure with Bubba grinned in pride as he escorted me into the church. I strolled arm and arm down the aisle with this uniformed solider; my debonair husband walked behind us in stoic support, as he had through the entire process.

Our being seated first that night allowed us to watch God's scene unfold. As the door's opened, and BJ and her father stepped in, I imagined what it would have been like to walk down the aisle with my father, but I felt sure he had continued to walk beside me long after I closed the door to that hospital room. BJ grinned and giggled as her eyes met Bubba's red face. Bubba shuffled his feet nervously, and we could hear him breathing "Whew," in an attempt to still his twittering heart. My wedding jewelry (BJ's "something borrowed") sparkled and flashed on her neck and wrist as she reached to kiss her crying father on the cheek.

As if in an inside, unspoken secret, Bubba glanced to us for calmness. I would shake my head "Yes" to him as if to say, "We know how badly you have wanted this. You have always spoken of finally having a family of your own. Yes, we are your family, and we will always be here, but now is your time to begin again."

As they poured their "unity sand" together into one beaker, I knew that their lives were now in God's hands. It was time for Jason and me to step away, try not to give advice unless asked (which would prove EXTREMELY hard to do for a control freak), and support them in their successes and failures.

We would stand beside Bubba in support of
his decision to start a new life.

Pouring their sand together denoted that their new life had begun.

After the Christmas holiday, they moved to Tennessee to be closer to Fort Campbell, Kentucky, where he was still stationed. Sometimes, they made decisions that scared us or were not the choice we would have made. We were not always wonderful at keeping our opinions to ourselves. Often, I thought I might need to put a binder clip on my lips when we would talk to them on the phone.

"So we traded my vehicle for something else and bought her a car too," he told me one night.

"Oh really? Well, if you think y'all can make it each month with your money, then you know best," I would answer. Now that was not my real answer, of course. It sounded more like, "AHHHHH! Are you crazy? How can you ever afford that?" But I wanted Bubba and BJ to continue to call us, right? So, I said what needed to be heard. They had not asked me what I thought anyway. (Which was their first mistake because surely Jason and I were wise and always made the right choices!)

On Mother's Day 2010, we received a phone call from the kiddos.

"Nia, we want to tell you something. We are going to have a baby!" Bubba told me while BJ giggled in the background.

A grandbaby? A grandbaby! I could not help but share in their excitement when I was on the phone with them, but when I got off the phone, the devil allowed worried thoughts to pop up like boiling bubbles:

"What if they have not been married long enough? What if he deploys after the baby is born? What if they have to move and we never get to see them and the baby? This is going to put such a strain on their new marriage. I wish they would find a church of their own while they are away."

The next morning, after little sleep, I was sick of myself. I was getting on my own nerves. I was allowing these stressors to become strongholds in my life in less than twenty-four hours after receiving what should have been joyous news.

"God, I am giving this to you. Here it is. I am laying it at Your feet. This is too heavy for me to bear, and You have told me that I don't have to live like this. Take care of Bubba, BJ, and this little peanut inside of her. Allow me to fully experience this blessing," I prayed.

"Casting all your cares upon Him, because He cares about you" (1 Peter 5:7, Holman Christian Standard). Yes, I had heard this scripture a million times and had known its effectiveness in my life, but sometimes, you just need to pick an old comfortable pair of shoes out of the closet, dust them off, and let your feet feel at ease. Immediately, I felt Him take the soaking wet net of worry I was dragging around and toss it back into the bottom of the sea of forgetfulness, where it belonged and would stay.

We were going to be thirty-year-old grandparents!

Chapter 33

*T*his grandmother-to-be was working on becoming the Bionic Woman. When I was twenty-five, I had made a trip back to the Muscular Dystrophy doctor in Birmingham. There was still no cure, but there was a surgery that would help stabilize my shoulder blades enough to raise my arms above my head. Well, call me a guinea pig! I was willing to do anything to help sword fight this disease. It had never been the definition of who I was nor would I allow it to be the ruler of what I would become.

My MD doctor referred me to an orthopedic surgeon also in Birmingham. A few meetings, a few tests, and these shoulder blades were going to get harnessed down! The surgery fell the summer after the one I had spent healing from my hysterectomy. The doctor would not repair both shoulders in one summer, so I would spend a third summer recovering from surgery the following year. It was not long into my stay at the hospital that I knew why he had refused to do two at once. WOW, that was some pain! If I had thought the tiny dancer on my ovaries was bad—then my shoulder blades were Tokyo being destroyed by Godzilla.

In a painful nutshell, the doctor had drilled holes in my shoulder blades, run wire through those holes, wrapped the wire around my rib cage, and pulled it down tight with a nice twist-tie motion like sealing a loaf of bread. He took a bone graph from my hip and packed it in around the scapula, then sewed me up!

The hospital stay was rough as the poor nurses and doctors struggled to find management for my pain. A morphine pump and an epidural later, I was still eating pain pills. All this was extremely hard on Jason; he broke down the first night when my pastor called to check on me.

"This is just so much worse than we thought it would be," he cried.

We made it through and, for months, poor Jason had to help take care of me as well as be the prime caretaker of the home, a duty we previously shared. I felt that I had put him through extra strain; however, I was so thankful that he shared my hope for a more physically capable future.

After months of physical therapy with the most godly therapists and assistants, my arm finally raised twice as high as it would originally. Now I would find it easier to wash my hair, write on the board, keep up a purse strap, and more importantly...PRAISE THE LORD!

We made it through the second surgery the following summer with equally successful results. These surgeries, blessings from God, allowed me to meet other women with my type of Muscular Dystrophy (Facioscapulohumeral). After having lunch and answering their questions about the details of the shoulder surgery, which they were considering, they told me of a surgery a friend had that had cured foot drop. If there would have been a surgeon in that restaurant where we were eating, I would have cleared the plates, thrown the biscuits and jelly in the floor, and screamed, "Someone hand him a butter knife!" I was ready for another surgery.

It became my mission to find a doctor who could perform the surgery. A renowned doctor in Chattanooga, Tennessee, was recommended by a friend who was a nurse. This doctor was not so easy to convince. He performed the surgery several times every month, but to perform a tendon transfer on a candidate with Muscular Dystrophy, that was a different story. Typically, this surgery helped patients who had suffered strokes or suffered paralysis. Tests, needles, and persuasion from his female secretaries (whom I had become friends with over so many appointments) finally convinced him I was the right person with which to take this chance.

The surgery could not have happened at a better time in my life. I was falling often, and such tumbles were beginning to become more painful. I fell and twisted my ankle at school.

One day, I fell going into a local store. As the years had gone by, it was difficult to just get up on my own. Of course, wouldn't you know that I had on a dress this day. So there I lay, at the front of the store, when the clerk, who was ringing up customers, looked at me.

"Oh hon, are you ok?"

"Yes ma'am, but I may have to have your arm to help me up," I said.

"Ok baby. Wait just a second until I get finished ringing up the customers."

"What? Huh? Sure, I'll just lay here and let everyone step over me who comes in the door. Yeah, you just take your time," I thought. I was humiliated. Typically, I could laugh off a fall, get up and curtsey, and limp off to lick my wounds later. Now, I was trying not to cry.

The manager came to find me in the floor waiting. She helped me up. "Oh Nia, are you sure you're ok? Oh, no! You're not pregnant are you?"

Well just go ahead and stab me while I'm down, please. Here, I was thinking I looked cute in my hot pink dress, but obviously it looked like a maternity dress to the rest of the world. I even had on my suck-in body shaper; unfortunately, when God was forming this wobbly body, He must have also thought it would be funny to give me lordosis, which causes your lower back to sway out, making your backside look huge and your front gut a twin with the back. With MD, you also have no stomach muscles, so my belly does pooch out making me look with child. I guess I'll never have to wonder what I would look like pregnant, right? Find the positives. Find the positives.

"Yes, yes, I'm fine. No, I'm not pregnant, just fat, I guess," I answered. "Please quit talking to me. Please quit talking. I'm trying not to cry. I need to get in an aisle and hide till I can get it together," I thought.

As I went into the school-supply aisle and had a moment of self pity, I turned around to see an old high school friend's father. Being around him reminded me so much of my own father. As we talked, our conversation drifted toward the Lord and what He had done in our lives. God had sent him to me, much like a red bird. I got the message: Do not focus on the few bad times in your life, Nia, focus on all the good I have given you.

Ok, so maybe this story makes what the foot doctor was about to say to me make sense: "You're vain, Nia. You seem to care about what kind of shoes you wear and how they are going to look with your outfit, but I am telling you that if you do have this tendon transfer, you will never be able to wear high heels again. You could risk stretching the tendons on the top of your feet and the surgery would have been for nothing. But if you listen to me and do as I say during your post care, you should be able to count on walking for several more years without having to worry about falling."

"I'm vain? I'm vain? Is it such a crime to avoiding wearing granny shoes with a dress? What? Never wear high heels again? What will I wear when I go to chaperone the prom? How could he say I'm vain?" These thoughts raced through my mind, but I gathered my cute shoes and threw them to the wayside.

"This disease has already robbed me in so many aspects. It has stolen the blessing of having children. It has taken away my ability to easily get in and out of the ocean to play while on vacation. It threatens to shorten my teaching career. As it stands now, I know what my future could be with MD. I have seen how it has taken my mother's independence away. I am more terrified of what I know my future holds than the possibility of what could come, or go wrong, with this tendon transfer surgery," I told the doctor.

He knew I was serious. I had spent months researching and talking to others with MD who also had the surgery. I was not going into this surgery blindly. When you have horrible balance, you never close your eyes for long.

I had the surgeries performed in the summer of 2010. (Yes, I barely knew what it was like to enjoy a teacher's summer). Being in a cast and a walking boot was not fun. Having bad balance to begin with, I was unable to walk on crutches and instead, strolled along with a walker. Although dragging that one hundred pound cast (exaggeration) around was misery, I could quickly tell that this surgery would be worth it.

When the cast was finally removed, my foot stuck straight into the air at attention. Before, it hung like a flower drooped by the soaking rain. I could have stared at my foot for hours!

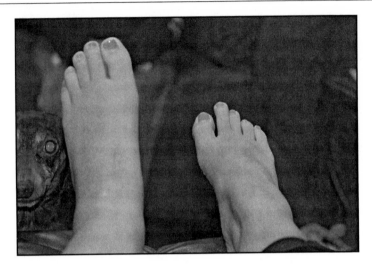

Here you can see the difference between my feet before (right) and after (left) the surgeries. (And you can see our weenie dog Penelope being nosey.)

I wear AFO (ankle-foot orthoses) right now. The doctor is making sure that my feet are healing properly. Yes, shoes are not as fun to shop for as they were previously. But I had to get real with myself. Just as I am not my disease, I am also not my clothes or shoes. Who cares? I have spent too much time in life worrying about insignificant circumstances.

God was about to remind me of the more important matters anyway.

Chapter 34

ecause of the surgeries, I was unable to start school with the other teachers. When I did start, I had to ride in an electric wheelchair in my classroom and in the halls. You guessed it—my worst fear—but somehow, now that I was facing the fear, it was not so scary anymore. I made the most of the wheelchair, and so did those high school students that I had to fight off. They all wanted to ride! Instead, I allowed them to decorate it with pompoms and come up with various personalized license plates. If there is one thing about teaching, it is this: kids make you laugh, and laughter is the best medicine. I was in pain at night, however. I had pushed myself too much during the day and was paying for it at night. It began to weigh on me mentally. I was becoming negative.

Occasionally, students are afflicted with an illness and are unable to come to school for a while. When this occurs, the school will ask a teacher to tutor them and be the go-between with their teachers, keeping up with their homework and grades.

There is nothing commendable in my reasoning to take on a homebound student in the fall of 2010. Jason and I could use the extra money, and tutoring was an opportunity to make it.

As I set the family's address into my GPS, I wondered what this seventh grade boy would be like. I had never had him in class, but I knew that he was very, very sick. He was unable to get up from his bed because doing so caused his eyes to blur and his head to swim. Often, that made him sick to his stomach. Not only was he suffering with this new condition, but he also had been ill, as a child, with a condition which caused his own immune system to be compromised. Weekly, his mother would receive a shipment of blood platelets, which would then be injected into him to help improve his immunity.

His mother had gorgeous fair skin, long auburn hair, and a sweet, compassionate smile. She led me through their beautiful home into his dimly-lit bedroom completely decorated with Alabama football memorabilia. He weakly looked up at me and squinted his eyes at the glow of the closet light behind me. I shook his hand and sat down to work. I attempted to loosen the moment with a few corny jokes, but I could tell that he did not feel like laughing. As I worked with him, I realized that the light from the closet was all he could bear. What was happening to him was much like a migraine; light seemed to aggravate it. He was unable to look at the words of his literature book, read the numbers in his math book, or write his answers on paper. I would need to talk him through every step of the way while writing down his answers. This was not going to be easy.

As I left that afternoon, his mother stepped onto the porch to tell me what they had just learned from the doctor. He had a tumor on his brain. In fact, there were two different spots. He had no idea what the doctor's news had been. They were going to tell him soon. I could tell that this mother of three, who tried to keep it all together for her family and husband, was crumbling under the pressure. She needed some help. I knew just where to find it. I asked her if I could pray for her. I grabbed the hands of this woman I had known only an hour and began to speak to the Healer. Another full circle moment for me, as I was now the teacher, and I was pushing aside my "desk" to step up to the throne on a student's behalf, as my former math teacher had done.

I found it hard to back out of their driveway that day. My eyes were too blurry. I had gone to this tutoring position for the purpose of money. I did not expect to find God waiting there in the living room of that house, poised to give me the gift of another life lesson. I did not deserve for Him to even interact with me when I was only there for such selfish reasons. I was broken at His goodness. Over and over, He loves me enough to nudge me along as a deer nudges her wobbly-legged fawn to stand. I deserved to have my feet knocked from under me. Instead, God was telling me to be strong for this family. "You have been blessed to have these surgeries. You will heal, in my time. This family needs you now. Focus on them for a while."

The next day, I did not seem to notice my aching feet or how the braces rubbed my legs. Shoes became no bother. In fact, I even got a pair of satin slippers to begin wearing as black dress shoes. Who cared? They worked, I was comfortable, and truth be known, other people probably wished they had on their slippers!

Over the next four months, this sweet family went through a horrible time being shuffled from doctor to doctor, sometimes hearing hopeful news, other times not. They were a faith-filled bunch. I was drawn to their belief that it was only a matter of time before they would see their miracle.

I have always believed that God has and can perform miracles. I had often seen Him work out situations in other's and my own life that I knew were nothing short of miraculous. When it came to praying for someone else's health, though, I mainly just prayed, "Your will be done, God, whether that is to heal or not, give us peace and Your grace to withstand this trial." Now, there may be nothing wrong with praying that way, but as I asked others to pray for my homebound student and saw the faith of his family, I encountered Christians who prayed with such power that I was sure I felt the walls shake. They knew that they had the power of the Holy Spirit living inside them—the same Spirit that raised Jesus from the dead. I began to realize that God *wants* to help, and He wants us to ask Him to do it. "But He was pierced for our transgressions, He was crushed for our iniquities; the punishment that brought us peace was on Him, and by His wounds we are healed" (Isaiah 53:5, New International Version). So I began to pray for that student and to ask God to heal him here on earth. I do not believe it was my prayers that made all of heaven stop to listen. However, I was part of a large mass of miracle-believing Christians who were insisting on heaven's silence while they cried out to the Lord.

After traveling to the Mayo Clinic in Minnesota, my student's mother sent a text: "It is a miracle! His tumor is gone!" Although I rejoiced when receiving this message, I worried that there had been a mistake or that possibly, the tumor would come back. Just call me Doubting Thomas, but I needed to see him for myself and wait for a little time to pass.

Week after week, we watched him build up strength. The tumor, which had been there when they arrived at the Mayo Clinic and was detected in the MRIs, was gone after performing the final MRI. The doctor attempted to explain but said he had no explanation.

"We know what happened," his family said.

The evidence was there, sitting in front of me on the couch, getting up to grab a pencil, working out math problems, and reading aloud science questions. It was not long before he was begging us to let him go back to school! We had to keep him at bay while he regained his strength. Goodness, he had been bed-ridden for four months! The last night of my tutoring was hard. I stayed way over my designated time. His mother and I rehashed the months we had been together along this journey. They had changed my life, and my outlook on miracles, and somehow, they said I had changed theirs. God is gracious.

He is back at school now. Sometimes, I will turn in the hallway and there he will be, grinning…that is right…like a 'possum. I will hug him and his trusty side-kick sister, and they will scuttle back down the hall.

"There goes my miracle," I'll say to myself.

Chapter 35

*O*n December 30, 2010, Bubba, BJ, and I loaded up and headed to Chattanooga, Tennessee, with our own personal labor and delivery nurse, my cousin. "Vayda," our grandbaby, would be born today. Jason would come to the hospital later. (You know, because he is not a control freak who has to be a part of every little detail.) Once in the hospital room, I thought of the months that had passed while we waited for our baby girl.

BJ had decided to live with us during the last six months of her pregnancy while Bubba had to go to Maryland for some Army training. It had been God's timing. She was there to help around the house and keep me company after my leg surgeries. As if it were not enough to have a son and now a daughter, I had been given almost as much time in our home with BJ as I had been given when Bubba was a senior. During those months, she and I had become very close. I enjoyed having some estrogen in the house, especially from a woman who was so calm and easy going. Together we stormed the TV, laughing at ridiculous reality stars and keeping sports from ruling in the Stivers' household. She and I handed out Halloween candy and put up holiday decorations. We solved the problems of the world and determined that life would be easier if everyone just agreed with us. I was with her when she learned we were having a girl baby. Together, we shopped for the first of many outfits for Vayda. Jason, BJ, and I made plans for that baby and imagined what she would look like. We were giddy about our granddaughter-to-be. BJ came to church, was in my Sunday School class, and went to Bible Study with me. As much as I looked forward to Vayda's birth, I also dreaded the time afterward because that meant BJ would move out to live with Bubba on his new post, Fort Hood, Texas. I was going to miss her. She, my very own daughter-in-law, had become a best friend.

BJ's birthing experience was long and strenuous. She did not progress as the doctor expected and that put pressure on her, the baby, and her surrounding family. At one point, the stress was too much. The doctor's options were frightening to us, when we were already tired. As BJ was finally resting, we, the waiting family, began to take our angst out on one another. Valerie suggested that we take our feelings to the Lord instead. We circled around BJ's hospital bed and held hands. I cried out to God for the safety of BJ and Vayda. I asked Him to grant us, as well as the doctors, wisdom and discernment. He was the God of details, and we needed Him to take care of everything.

As I prayed, peace fell on that room. Our hearts became calm; our tensions relaxed. I knew that God had heard our plea, and He was already beginning His answer.

Vayda was born, on December 31 instead of the 30th, after twenty-seven hours of labor including three hours of pushing. Our four-foot-eleven daughter had been so strong. Vayda, unfortunately, suffered trauma during the long process, and when the doctor helped her into the world, she was not breathing.

He did not hold her up for us to admire. He did not lay her on BJ's chest for those first precious moments. She was whisked to the table where the neonatal intensive care nurses began to work on her. An oxygen mask covered her tiny face. Her unresponsive body rocked violently as they rubbed and stimulated her flesh. Her legs and arms lay lifelessly to the side of her body. There was no cry. Her limbs did not resist the nurses who were holding them. God placed one of our church friends in the room, unexpectedly, that day. She was also a NICU nurse who had not been scheduled to work. That detail may seem insignificant, but My God lives in the details. (Remember, what I prayed around the bed?) Our friend's eyes darted to Valerie. "Pray! Y'all need to pray!" she mouthed.

Bubba collapsed onto BJ's stomach. He wailed out at the sterile air. Then, he turned and fell onto Jason, soaking his shirt with tears. While I stood in shock, looking at this baby we had made plans for and dreamed about, I could not move or begin to speak.

Valerie grabbed my head and mashed my face to hers, "Oh precious Heavenly Father, we come to you now..."

"She's breathing! She's ok!" Valerie was interrupted by the reassuring excitement of our friend. (I would always wonder, had our nurse friend not been there to tell us to pray, what would have happened in that moment? I was glad our friend's schedule had been supernaturally changed.)

Vayda squeaked out in agreement. It was the most beautiful sound I have ever heard.

I slowly walked up to the side of the table, and for the first time, laid my eyes fully upon my granddaughter. She was everything we dreamed of. I stroked her tiny arm, and her hand clasped around my fingertip.

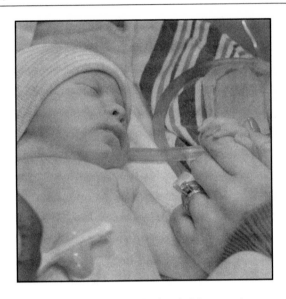

Holding her hand while she's holding my heart.

Bubba looked at me and revealed that her name was "Vayda Nicole." Nicole is my middle name. Jason stood behind me, his hand caressing my shoulder, and we stared back at this room—at all God had given us. Oh, He is too good. We have surely done nothing to deserve this steady flow of blessings He has poured out upon us.

But God, in His infinite love, had kept His promises to that little eleven-year-old whose weak legs swung back and forth as her parents received the news of their daughter's disease. The Savior had given her the gift of His son when she was fifteen. The Prince of Peace was faithful to a lonely college girl and had loved her enough to bring her to her knees at the foot of His cross. Jehovah Jireh helped her say goodbye to her daddy and hello to her godly husband. The Comforter had taught that barren woman to sing a new song in preparation for the children, and grandchildren, He would one day give her. Yes, His promise had come true and was continuing to be fulfilled:

"'For I know the plans I have for you,' declares the Lord. 'Plans to prosper and not to harm you, plans to give you hope and a future" (Jeremiah 29:11, New International Version).

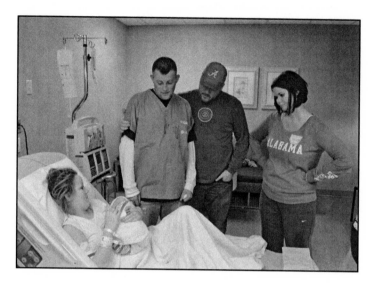

God had completed us.

Epilogue

I have always known I would write a book one day. But when the opportunity presented itself, it took a little persuading from the Lord before I began to obey. (Ok, so it took a scream in the face from God.)

Remember those same sorority sisters I used to party with? Well, in September of 2010, we attended a Christian women's conference together. God had brought us all full circle. As we leafed through our weekend itinerary, my friend paused, looked at me, and held up her program.

"This is you, Nia. It's your time. You have GOT to do this," she demanded. (She was really a little pushy about it, in fact.)

I read the words across the page that she was sticking in my face: "Everyone has a story to share. What's yours?" it read.

A writing competition. A chance to be published. A chance to finally write a book.

I felt like I had been punched in the stomach. For the rest of the weekend, my mind tossed around the idea. "Was this *really* my time?"

I couldn't wait to get home to talk to Jason about it.

"Do it," he said. "You know I've always told you that you would write a book one day."

"What if I'm not old enough? What if God gives me much more, and I'm supposed to wait for that? What if I lose in the contest? How will I handle that since the writing will be so personal to me? How will I break up the chapters? What exactly am I going to write about?" I could have questioned aloud on and on, but Jason was losing interest in my rambling. Heck, my own mind couldn't keep up with itself.

That night at church, I decided I would just sit on the pew and pray instead of going to the altar. If I went to the altar, I might have to tell my dilemma to someone who would come to pray with me. What if they thought I was crazy? (Now, please know that I am never secretive about anything. My life is usually an open book. [No pun intended.] Somehow though, I got the vibe from God that this impending decision was not to be shared with everyone. That verse, "But Mary treasured up these things and pondered them in her heart," came to mind. [Luke 2:19, New International Version])

I sat on the front pew and bowed my head, alone. Suddenly, one of my best friends was beside me, her head on top of my head. I was at a loss for words. I needed her to pray with me.

"I'm trying to pray about being obedient," I whispered. "I don't know if God is telling me to write a book for this competition or not. I feel like I'm being led in that direction, but I need a sign or something."

"Remember the story our pastor told us? The man was sitting on the roof of his house during a flood, waiting for God to send a miracle. A boat came by and offered him a ride. He refused because he was waiting for God. A helicopter flew over. He wouldn't get on because he was waiting on God's miracle. He died and went to heaven. He said, 'God, why didn't you save me?' and God said, 'I tried! I sent a boat and a helicopter!' Nia, how many signs will it take before you realize God is asking you to be obedient? I wish that you had heard a sermon our pastor just gave at another church. It was about obedience. You need it," she said.

I asked my pastor about the sermon. A few weeks later he preached it. I died inside. I knew that I was supposed to step out, have faith, and start writing.

I went home that day after church and typed. Another Sunday, I typed more. Then, I stopped. I still felt convicted, but I used excuses: "I have writer's block. I don't know where to go from where I am," or "I don't want to write with Bubba and BJ home. We have such a short time with them." Yeah, yeah. I was just being lazy. I just wasn't picking up the computer—well, except to peruse the Internet.

I felt horrible about it. Every stinkin' time I went to church I felt like there was a giant book sitting on the stage, staring right at me. How rude! I mean, the nerve of some books! One day, I even went to the altar and told God I was sorry and would begin writing again.

Do you ever feel really "spiritual" at church and then lose that feeling right when you walk out the door? God was patient...then. He just kept nudging.

When I watched TV, someone mentioned writing a book. "In my book, I write about my experiences," someone being interviewed on the radio would say. I sat beside a woman at a basketball game whose relative had just...da...da...daaaa...published a book! Book, book, book! It was beginning to feel like that weird scene in *Dumbo* where all the elephants are multiplying and marching all over the screen.

I was thankful, to be honest, that only Jason, my friend, Mama, and Valerie knew I was even considering the competition. As God would have it, they did not even ask about how it was coming along. I believe that He wanted to be the one who prodded me. I'm glad though. When I did cave in, it was because I did not want to disappoint God, not everyone else.

Here's how the caving in, I mean, sink hole, happened. At the beginning of the spring semester, I was sitting in my classroom during my planning period. I wasn't too busy—yet—because I had no papers to grade and all my necessary beginning-of-the-semester tasks were completed. I couldn't believe it. I was caught up. That never happens to teachers. God wanted it to happen. I was bored, actually. Suddenly, a strong thought came over me: "Open up that book on your desk and read the first paragraph."

"Now why would I do that? I read that book five years ago. It is only on my desk because I pulled it off the shelf the other day to show the kids an example and forgot to put it back." I was reasoning with myself.

"Open the book and read the first paragraph!" The thought was louder and more persistent.

"Alright, alright, but this is really silly."

I read the first line. The author was at his mailbox when his neighbor walked up and asked him how his book was coming along. The author said he didn't have the heart to tell her that he hadn't even started it yet.

I dropped the book. Now, that was a little too freaky. "I hear you God! I get it now!"

I immediately whirled around in my chair and began typing. I was too scared not to. What was God's next prompt? A lightning bolt? I definitely did not need that. This hair was frizzy enough.

I poured out two chapters that day. I began to write a little more every day. I was thankful that I was writing, at least, but could I ever meet the deadline? At this point, I had really made things hard for myself. Now, after knowing about the competition for four months, I only had eleven days. But hey, I was working with the Creator of the Universe here. He created everything in seven days. Surely, He could take care of a little book if I'd just keep my fingers typing!

The book became all I could think about. I imagined chapters and events that I would include. Ideas came to me quickly. It was easy when the weight of the world wasn't on your shoulders anymore. It feels good being obedient to God.

The news channels reported the same information. Fellow Bridgeport-ians ran out and bought all the milk and bread they could find. A snow like we had not seen in eighteen years was headed our way. With six days left until the competition deadline, snow fell in such masses that the news called it "thunder snows." We had seven to eight inches in one night. (I know to all those people who live in snow 360 days a year that it might not sound like much, but to those of us who live in the South, we were snowed in—unless you had a four-wheel drive.) As a result of those little snowflakes—my friends—we were out of school for the ENTIRE WEEK! AHHH! Go on, God! He was moving mountains of snow on my behalf! I could "hole up" and write nonstop in preparation to meet that deadline.

My mind fell blank on Monday. I stared at the blinking curser. It surely wasn't doing any work to help me out. I looked to our weenie dogs, Penelope and Oscar. No help there. Jason was gone. He was out building an eleven-foot snowman in the churchyard with some of our church family.

"Please God," I begged. "I need wisdom. I need discernment. I need something! I'm stuck!"

Just then, the phone rang. I looked down at the caller ID to see WestBow Press, the name of the publishing company who was sponsoring the competition. ARE YOU KIDDING ME, GOD? THIS IS TOO COOL!

Speaking of cool, that's how I tried to act when I answered the phone. Sure, I speak to a publishing company every day. I immediately began to sweat in my fleece pink and purple polka dotted pajama pants.

The consultant was calling to check on me and to see if I had any questions about the competition. We talked for twenty minutes! He was my new best friend! In the middle of discussing my writing ideas and my writer's block, he began to pray. There was no "Can I pray for you?" or "I'm about to pray for you," just a "Heavenly Father, I come to you on behalf of Nia…" He prayed for the chapter I was stuck on, and he prayed for my work during the week before the deadline. He asked God to bless me and speak to me. I was, on the other end of the line, dying. I grabbed my mouth and tried not to let him know that I had broken into the "ugly cry." He sensed my emotion when he finished his prayer.

"Nia, you have a sweet spirit. I can tell it even over the phone. You also have a confidence about your writing. I believe you are doing the right thing. I believe God has asked you to write and you are obeying Him." I was overwhelmed. God was touching me on the shoulder again. As if I needed any more direction that I was supposed to be writing, God was still letting me know that He was pleased with my obedience. Wow, I wanted to feel like that forever.

After we got off the phone (and I called and screamed to my mom and sister on three-way calling), I was able to write like a mad woman. All week, I burned that keyboard up. As I began to think back over the years, God revealed more and more how He had worked behind the scenes in my life. I felt so honored that He would even let me look through His rearview mirror. Years before I ever knew anything about Him, he had already set into motion a conveyor belt that would bring me to Him. He was in love with me and was wooing me to Himself.

I did not, however, win the competition. To be honest, I was absolutely devastated when I saw the postings on the internet. I reacted as if God had never taken His own mysterious path in my life where I just had to close my eyes, hold on to Him, and hang on. Duh, Nia, like you weren't serving a God who had ALWAYS been faithful before! The control freak in me had kicked in again because the path I thought He would choose had not been chosen, and I had no idea where we were going!

"God, how could Your hand be in this so strongly only for me to become broken hearted?" It made no sense to me. My heart knew God's promises while my head began to be attacked by the devil's lies.

"You're not good enough. The story God has given you isn't worthy. You're nothing. You're a failure." Two days worth of the devil running his mouth, and I was driven to my knees at the altar. I would not stand for this. My God was the author and finisher of my life. He had yet to write a bad chapter. Every time I thought my life was cursed by circumstances, He had turned those ashes to beauty. No, my story *was* good enough because God wrote it.

I spent a few weeks in fervent prayer while I searched through scripture for an answer. During that time I learned that God requires sacrifice from us; however, the sacrifice is not what is important to God. It's the obedience that comes with the sacrifice. I obeyed God when He told me to write the book. It took a sacrifice of time, for sure. He never promised me that just because I obeyed, I would win the competition. So many times, my students will say, "If I study for this test and do well, what will I get?" Often, they ask as I'm giving homework, "Is this for a grade?" We are like that with God. We want to know, "What's in it for me if I do this, God?" Just like with my students, maybe the answer is the same with God. "You get to learn. You get to grow and become better." Our ultimate goal as Christians, remember, is to become more like Christ. Isn't that the best reward anyway? Yeah, I know, it is easy to say but sometimes it is hard to remember when you are asking, "Why, God?"

I could not shake off the feeling that this story God had given me was meant to help others who were hurting and questioning. I kept listening. I continuously pressed God for answers as to what next step I should take with the book. The answer came, tucked in the words of a Max Lucado weekly devotion that Valerie had emailed me as he explained how he had been rejected fifteen times before publishing. During Sunday School, the same sweet friend who had prayed with me at the beginning of my journey and had reminded me of the man waiting for a sign on the rooftop of his house said, "I believe God blesses us with certain gifts or events in our life to share with others and bless them. If we don't use those for Him, I believe He will take them away."

I decided to press forward to publish the book. God has blessed my life. Over and over and over again, He has poured His faithful love upon me. This book is the least I can do for Him. I so desperately want for its readers to find what they are searching for stashed in the pages because He has plans to give you "hope and a future" (Jeremiah 29:11).

Although I have felt blessed as I have looked back over my life while writing this book, I believe that anyone could begin to reflect on how God has worked out His plans for them. You may have been a Christian from childhood; take time to think of how He has taught you more about Himself along the way. If you were a "late bloomer" as I was, it is pretty neat to realize how He was jumping up and down to get your attention. If you have yet to give Him a glance, stop and look closer. His hands formed you. How can He not be in love with you? It was His breath that you breathed out in your first cry. You were created to love and worship Him. Friend, let me tell you (as if you haven't already read it), you don't know what you're missing. Accepting Christ will cost you nothing, but in return you'll gain so much to help you through this world while also receiving a stamped ticket to a better world where legs will run strong, daddies won't die, and past sinners will receive a crown. This deal has no drawbacks. There is no fine print. The dotted line has already been signed in His blood. Just hold out your hand and watch what plans He will unfold for your life.

Lord, I lay this book, my crown of Your glory, at Your feet...

References

The Holman Illustrated Study Bible. Nashville, TN: Holman Bible Publishers, 2006.

The Holy Bible, New International Version. The Grandmother's Bible. Grand Rapids, MI: International Bible Society, 2008.

The Message: The Bible in Contemporary Language. Women of Faith. Eugene H. Patterson. Colorado Springs, CO: NavPress, 2008.

9 781449 715571